THE ANCIENT GREEK
AND ROMAN THEATRE

Consulting Editor: ALN S. DOWNER

RANDOM HOUSE *New York*

PETER D. ARNOTT

Tufts University

The
Ancient Greek and
Roman Theatre

ISBN: 0-394-31471-9

DEC 13 71
Library of Congress Catalog Card Number: 70-146501

Manufactured in the United States of America by H. Wolff Book Mfg. Co., New York.

987654321
First Edition

Acknowledgments

The translations from Greek and Latin works are the author's throughout. The author and publisher acknowledge their thanks for permission to reproduce passages from the following:

From Aeschylus, *Agamemnon, The Oresteia: Part I* and *The Libation Bearers* and *The Eumenides, The Oresteia: Parts II* and *III*, translated and edited by Peter D. Arnott. Copyright 1964 by Meredith Publishing Company. Reprinted by permission of Appleton-Century-Crofts, Educational Division, Meredith Corporation.

From Aristophanes, *The Clouds* and Plautus, *The Pot of Gold*, translated and edited by Peter D. Arnott. Copyright © 1967 by Meredith Publishing Company. Reprinted by permission of Appleton-Century-Crofts, Educational Division, Meredith Corporation.

From *Three Greek Plays for the Theatre: The Medea and Cyclops of Euripides, The Frogs of Aristophanes,* translated and edited by Peter D. Arnott. Copyright © 1961 by Indiana University Press. Reprinted by permission of Indiana University Press.

Contents

THE ANCIENT GREEK
AND ROMAN THEATRE

Introduction

It is unfortunately and invariably true that we know the least about those theatres that existed during the periods of theatre history whose plays we are most interested in. It is particularly true, and particularly unfortunate, in the case of Greece in the fifth century B.C., the period of the theatre's first great flowering and of the creation of a vital part of the world's dramatic legacy; we have the texts of more than forty plays but know next to nothing about the technical resources with which they were produced. This gap in our knowledge has been doubly harmful. Our ignorance of the staging conditions has contributed to the aura of remoteness, of other-worldliness, that has hung over Greek drama for centuries, particularly in educational circles, and has effectively prevented generations of students and audiences from comprehending its immediacy, pungency, and raw theatricality. And at the same time, the few scraps of solid information that we do possess are subject to widely different interpretations—influenced, usually, by the theatrical conditions prevailing in the scholar's own time—which breed rancorous partisanship among the specialists and bafflement among the neophytes. Perhaps no area of classical scholarship has produced so much academic acrimony as the reconstruction of the Greek theatre of the fifth century B.C. Was it originally square or round? Did it provide a raised platform for its actors or not? Was it little more than a demarcated area for dancing, or was it, as some German scholars have preferred to think, a virtual Greek archetype of Wagner's Bayreuth, hung with canvas scenery and bristling with mechanical contrivances? Such fundamental issues remain substantial areas of controversy into which archaeologists, textual critics, social historians, and practical men of the theatre have flung the weight of their authority.

For the state of our ignorance we have mainly the Greeks to blame. The theatrical historian—unless he is fortunate enough to be working in Japan, where the living past is constantly before his eyes—must be guided largely by written testimony. And such information does not exist for the Greek period. It is not merely that time has obliterated it; it was just not written down in the first place. True, some books were written. Sophocles wrote a monograph, *On the Chorus,* which, given the Greek habit of making the word "chorus" virtually synonymous with "play," may have been wider in scope than the title immediately suggests. It has been argued, indeed, that what Sophocles wrote was a textbook on all aspects of play production. Yet Aristotle—surely the most widely read man of his time—implicitly denies this when he remarks, a century later, that no one before him has written on acting, although it is a subject of the greatest importance. It is an additional irritation that Aristotle himself contributes little to our knowledge in this area.

We must regret, too, the loss of certain comedies by Aristophanes, which gave an insider's view of the workings of the tragic theatre and would have taught us much through parody; those which survive provide some valuable clues. For the fourth century, we would like to have the study of delivery attributed to Theophrastus. But the systematic studies belong to a later period. King Juba's comprehensive history of the theatre, now lost but drawn upon extensively by Pollux, was written when the plays of Aeschylus, Sophocles, and Euripides were already "classics" and had largely vanished from the living repertory.

Why were the books not written? Because, in a small and orally oriented society, the need for the technical monograph had not yet arisen; because theatre was, as yet, in no sense "big business," but based on a master-disciple relationship in which training must have been primarily by word of mouth and example; because the Greeks felt no necessity to record a feature of their lives familiar to all as spectators, and to many as participants, for the choruses were drawn from the citizen body at large. We lack the comments of visiting foreigners that enliven our view of, for example, the Elizabethan public playhouse. And, finally, because the Greek theatre with its limited activity—two or three weeks of performances each year—was largely tradition-bound. The modern theatre is cross-fertilized from a multiplicity of sources and subject to an infinite variety of influences that require to be catalogued and analyzed. The Greeks by and large clung to an established pattern until it was destroyed by its own practitioners. There were changes, but they took longer to occur and were often fiercely resisted; innovations that would probably seem trivial to us became major areas of controversy for the Greeks. So far as the physical theatre was concerned, Euripides was using the same technical resources at the end of the fifth century that Aeschylus had used near the beginning. There was no need to explain the familiar.

The nature of the evidence may be summarized as follows. Our knowledge of the later Greek theatre—that which entertained the audiences of Alexander's time and their descendants—

is fairly substantial, based both on archaeological evidence and written testimony. Our knowledge of the earlier period, in which we are chiefly interested, is mostly intelligent surmise from a variety of sources. These are mainly the following.

1. Archaeological excavations, which yield impressive results for the fourth century B.C. and later, but which are of little value for the fifth century. Most of the ancient theatres surviving in Greece today—many of which are still used for summer revivals of classical plays—date from the Hellenistic period. It is logical to suppose that they preserved many features of the earlier buildings, or translated the temporary wooden structures of Sophocles' time into the permanence of stone, but the exact nature of this inheritance is arguable. The scanty stone survivals from the fifth century will be discussed in Chapter One.

2. Written accounts of the later Greek and Graeco-Roman theatres. There are two works of major importance: the architectural treatise composed by Vitruvius in the first century A.D. with a long section on theatres, and that portion of the *Onomasticon* by the lexicographer Pollux, written a century later, dealing with theatrical terminology. These vary from the laboriously detailed to the infuriatingly vague—the latter, particularly, in descriptions of stage machinery, which have inspired arguments from the Renaissance to our own time. Once again, these books tell us a good deal about the later theatre, but the extent to which these descriptions can be applied to the earlier structures is debatable. We know of several important changes from the fifth century theatre to that which Vitruvius describes; there may have been more than we suspect.

3. The plays themselves. These are virtually devoid of stage directions—the Greekless reader should be warned more often than he is that the directions in his English versions usually come from the translator and have no authority in the original—but often contain significant indications of stage behavior and scenic requirements.

4. The later commentaries (*scholia*) on the plays by Greek, Alexandrian, or Byzantine scholars. We possess a large accumula-

tion of these, assiduously copied with the texts themselves from one manuscript to another. Many concern setting, acting, and production, and obviously derive from eyewitness reports. The difficulty lies with our not knowing to which period to assign them, or whether the scholiast's comment refers to the original production or to a revival perhaps centuries later.

5. Vase paintings of theatres and scenes from productions, or at least inspired by such productions. This evidence is valuable, because the vase painters, prolific workers, were concerned with capturing anything that was in the public eye, and the stage was a rich source of material. The problem for the scholar here is to distinguish between the demands of different media and decide whether at any given moment the artist is reproducing the scenic conventions of the theatre or employing pictorial conventions of his own. Many illustrations are certainly suggestive; though to argue, as some scholars have done, that the vases uniformly and faithfully reproduce what the spectator could see on the stage is preposterous.

There are other, minor sources: stray references and passing comparisons, sometimes found in the most unlikely places. The historian's task is to fit these into a plausible and workable whole, the exact nature of which must inevitably vary with the individual and his times. The Greek theatre as seen by Manzius was not that as seen by Haigh, with whom Pickard-Cambridge differed as radically as I have with Pickard-Cambridge. In one respect, perhaps, the present generation of scholars is more fortunate. Even with the best will in the world, total objectivity is impossible; our vision of the theatres of the past is necessarily colored by what we see in our own. But our own age has rediscovered the arena and the values of the open stage, and our conception of the Greek theatre may have a somewhat greater validity than that formulated in a century whose stages were still bounded by the drop curtain and proscenium arch.

With the Roman theatre we are in the same predicament as with the Greek. For the period in which we are most interested— the two generations represented by Plautus and Terence, who brought the later Graeco-Roman comedy to its full development —our knowledge of production conditions is negligible. Archaeology is of no help, because Rome, though it produced a string of distinguished playwrights, had no permanent theatre of its own until a century after Terence's death. For the temporary, makeshift structures of the second century B.C., we are limited to guesswork based on the contemporary Greek theatres, on the plays themselves, and on passing allusions in contemporary or later authors. Again as with the Greek, the amount of information increases as the quality of the writing diminishes. The theatres and amphitheatres of the Roman Empire have survived in quantity, in Rome itself, the Italian cities, and the provinces. The Roman edifice at Arles is still a working playhouse, as Epidauros is in Greece. We are able to reconstruct the slaughters, spectacles, and beast shows at the Colosseum in almost indecent detail. But the stage on which Plautus' *farceurs* strutted, and Terence's more introspective comic heroes philosophized, is only vaguely perceived through half-comprehended allusions, distorted medieval renderings, and tentative analogies.

The present volume attempts to provide a working outline of the history and mechanics of the Greek and Roman theatre, both as a historical introduction for the student of theatre and literature, who should see plays against the background for which they were written, and as a guide to the director, who, even if he wishes to go off in new directions, should at least know what he is departing from. It tries to be honest in indicating where doubt and controversy lie, but seeks at the same time not to obfuscate by introducing more details of such controversy than the average student needs.

◻

CHAPTER ONE

The
Greek Theatre:
Origins and Development

Greek Theatre Building

Of the many theories about the origins of Greek drama, the one held by the Greeks themselves remains the most plausible: that the nucleus of the drama was the chorus, whose performances evolved from narration of familiar legends to a dramatic reenactment of such stories in song and dance. In the same way it is likely that the nucleus of the Greek theatre building was its characteristic feature, the *orchestra* (literally "dancing place"; the modern sense is a much later derivation), where the chorus performed. The theatre, then, starts with an arena. Of what shape? One school of thought finds its origins in the Cycladic civilization, which preceded that of Greece proper, and the rectangular "theatral areas," which are prominent features of the Minoan palaces of Crete. Excavations at Knossos on the north coast of the island and Phaistos on the south have uncovered two impressive examples, virtually identical in their general structure. They are surrounded by tiers of steps. Knossos has, in addition, what appears to be a "royal box" and a ceremonial entranceway into the arena. Fragmentarily preserved Cretan frescoes show spectators ranged on stone bleachers, which may well represent structures like these. They are enjoying a spectacle at whose nature we can only guess, for though we still have the arenas, we have little idea what went on in them. Certainly no Cretan dramatic literature has yet been discovered. The "theatral areas" may have been used for dances, processions, or the bullfights, which formed an important part of Cretan religious ritual. It has been argued that the earliest *orchestras* on the Greek mainland followed the same rectangular outline, and that the more familiar circle was a later development. This theory, once derided, has received additional support from recent excavations. Traces of what appear to be a rectangular arena have been discovered among the earliest strata of buildings on the Athenian Acropolis, north of the Erechtheum.

Another theory, more widely accepted, argues that the circular form was employed in Greece from the beginning. In this case, the probable exemplar would be the circular stone-paved threshing floor, to this day a familiar sight in any Greek village. The theory is an attractive one, for it suggests a primitive origin for the choral performances in the natural seasonal activities of the people. Around these threshing floors the community would gather after the harvest and enliven the tedium of their work with song, which would also placate the fertility gods whose patronage they sought. We may imagine a gradual transition from these spontaneous outpourings to a formal art which still embodied the community spirit, from rhythmical movement to dance-drama. Such excursions into the drama's origins, however, must remain hypothetical. We know only that the form of the threshing floor was also the form of the later *orchestra*. The circular shape became standard and dictated the pattern of the theatre as a whole.

As in the formative stages of any art, the original performers were improvisers, utilizing existing facilities as best they could. With the development of performances organized at the civic level, a need arose for more appropriate surroundings. We may trace, in Athens, the steps whereby a semipermanent performance center was created. The earliest *orchestra* of which we have any information was located in the *agora,* or market place, the city's business, administrative, and social center. Another was subsequently built on the slope of the Acropolis, in the precincts of the Temple of Dionysos. This deity, imported from the East, was at first primarily a fertility god. He rapidly assumed other functions, the most important being his patronage of the fledgling drama. In Athens, as elsewhere, the theatre building retained its intimate connection with the center of Dionysiac worship, a connection that persisted even with the growing secularization of the drama and the elaboration of theatre architecture: in Pergamon, in Asia Minor, the fourth-century theatre was still conceived as part of the temple complex. Even where theatres were dedicated to other, local deities—as at Oropos, to the hero Amphiaraos, or at Epidauros, to the semidivine healer Asklepios—the spirit of Dionysos was still strongly present. In Athens the relocation of the *orchestra* had one great practical advantage. It permitted far greater numbers of people to watch the performance from the steep hillside. The spectators sat on the ground at first, later on wooden bleachers, and finally, as the theatre became grander (or, according to one account, because the wooden seats collapsed in mid-performance), on concentric tiers of stone seats following the circular shape of the *orchestra* and the natural contours of the terrain. The Greeks had come naturally to one of the classic methods of seating a large number of spectators around a small space. It was not unique to them—similar theatres, of an early date, have been discovered in Peru—but it remained the characteristic pattern of Greek and, with certain modifications, of Roman theatre building.

We are chiefly concerned with the Theatre of Dionysos in Athens, for it was here that the works of Aeschylus, Sophocles, Euripides, Aristophanes, and Menander were first performed. The ruins remain, though they are encrusted by accretions; the most prominent features of the theatre as it now exists date from the reign of Nero, in the first century A.D. Some traces of the earliest structure survive, however, to show how the original *orchestra* was subsumed into a larger complex. A few stones, marking the rim of the circle, provide the earliest evidence of theatre building. The center of the *orchestra* was presumably marked, then as later, by an altar, symbolic of the drama's religious associations and serving also as a convenient focal point for the patterns of the choral dance. There are suggestions that the flute player or chorus leader (*coryphaios*) used its stepped base as an elevation. On the surrounding hillside, the spectators enclosed the performance almost completely; it was theatre-in-the-round.

The evolution of the actor proper, as distinct from the singing and dancing chorus, created new architectural problems. Who was responsible for this vital creative step, which made drama out of semidramatic narrative, is not known. The Greeks had their own theory. They attributed the innovation to one Thespis, who, in some versions, was an inspired chorister who took it upon himself to assume an individual part and respond to the chorus: thus the literal meaning of the Greek word for actor, *hypokrites* ("answerer"). It seems equally likely, however, that Thespis was an exponent of an independent dramatic non-choral tradition. Scattered references mention his taking performances through the countryside, using a cart or trestle platform as a stage. The Greeks honored him as the founder of their drama and established the date of his first performance at the Athenian festival as 534 B.C., under the auspices of the autocrat Peisistratos. This tradition undoubtedly simplifies a long and complex historical process. We know of other early types of equally influential semidramatic activity, but it is safe to see the genesis of the drama proper either in the evolution of individual performers from the choral school or in the combination of separate acting and choral traditions. The tyrant Peisistratos had a mixed reputation among ancient historians; but if he truly lent his authority to this new type of celebration—which, as we know, was frowned on by some traditionalists—he justified his existence.

The introduction of the actor gave Greek drama its characteristic structure—an alternation of acted scenes (*episodes*) and choral song—and a new element to the physical theatre. There was now need of a place where the soloist could retire between appearances and change costume as required; a place, too, to set him off from the chorus and act as a sounding board for his voice. As in the case of the *orchestra,* its precise origins remain hypothetical. Perhaps it was Thespis' cart, drawn up on the rim of the *orchestra,* that became the first scene house. The technical vocabulary of the Greek theatre suggests that the early structures were of rudimentary simplicity. *Skene,* the name the Greeks gave to the scene house, the actor's place, means literally "hut," "tent," "booth." One improbable theory suggests that the original *skene* was the actual tent of Xerxes, which was captured at the battle of Salamis in 480 B.C.

The word was preserved in use long after the theatres were transformed to stone: stage practice has a way of retaining terms which have lost their original significance. Through the Latin transliteration *scaena,* we get our word "scene": it is important to note, however, that the original *skene* was in no sense what we now mean by scenery. It was intended not to depict any specific place demanded by the action but simply to provide a background against which the actors could perform. A more recent theory suggests another possible origin for the *skene,* in the architecture of the shrines in whose precincts the plays were performed, using an existing wall pierced with niches for the display of divine effigies as a neutral facade against which the action could unfold.

In the Greek theatre as we know it, the *skene* appears as an appendage, an adjunct, breaking the perfect circularity of the design. The Theatre of Dionysos shows how this addition took semi-permanent form. Adjoining the rim of the earliest *orchestra*-circle is a rough stone foundation pierced with slots. These presumably carried uprights for a wooden *skene* facade. Most archaeologists would date this foundation at about 450 B.C., that is, roughly about the time of the production of the *Oresteia*. In the theatre of the great commercial city of Corinth, almost as old as that of Athens, a system of stone sockets set into the natural slope of the land suggests a similar arrangement. The earliest building here has been dated about 415 B.C. Literary references suggest that this type of semipermanent structure survived in use for some considerable time. Dismantled when the dramatic festivals were over, it permitted the use of the area for other purposes: in Athens, the *orchestra* also served as a booksellers' market. At Thorikos, a tiny village under Athenian jurisdiction, the excavations show a complex system of holes in a rough stone wall, designed to support a

Athens, Theatre of Dionysos.
Earliest stone foundations for the *skene*.

wooden facade on an inconveniently steep slope. The Hellenistic Theatre of Pergamon was forced to retain such an arrangement because the *skene* lay across the processional entrance to the Temple of Dionysos. In consequence, the whole structure was made transportable and erected at need in sockets sunk into the terrace level.

It seems, then, that contemporaneously with the emergence of its first major playwright, the theatre had already assumed the shape it was to retain, without serious modification, for more than a century. The pattern we have observed at Athens and Corinth was standard throughout Greece, though local conditions caused certain variations, particularly in size. Conservative estimates give the Theatre of Dionysos in Athens 17,000 spectators, Corinth 15,000, and Epidauros 14,000, while at the local cult-center of Oropos the theatre holds a few hundred only. It is important to remember, however, that the major playwrights wrote with the larger theatres in mind, and that the size of the audience established certain prerequisites for both writing and performance. For some idea of the problems involved, we might compare the Greek theatre to a bullring or a football stadium: it has much more in common with these structures than with the theatre of today. Most of the spectators sat at a considerable distance from and looked down upon the performance: their sightlines were not ours, and the amount of detail they could be expected to perceive was limited. We shall return to these considerations later.

Sometimes the intractability of the terrain meant that the builders could only approximate the ideal pattern. This is particularly true of Thorikos, a rough-and-ready structure which may, indeed, be the oldest known theatre. Here we have, as already noted, a makeshift *skene* supported with difficulty on the uncompromising rock; a trapezoidal *orchestra*, which seems to owe its shape to the natural contours of the land; and an auditorium which follows the outline of the *orchestra*, virtually rectangular in shape, though curving at the ends. We may surmise that the theatre at Thorikos was built with local labor and limited resources, making the most of difficult conditions. At the other end of the scale, we may look at the Theatre of Epidauros, a professionally designed theatre in an ideal site. Although not built until the fourth century, it retains the full circular *orchestra* of the fifth. Still in use for annual festivals of ancient drama, it is a fine working example of the ancient theatre at its prime, demonstrating the unique conditions for which the Greek playwright wrote.

Relation of Audience to the Performance

We have described the fifth-century theatre loosely as theatre-in-the-round. To all intents and purposes, this was true. Part of the rim of the *orchestra* was occupied by the *skene*, framed between the processional entranceways (*parodoi*) which brought the chorus into the *orchestra*. The rest of the space was taken up by spectators. They surrounded the performance almost completely, and the orchestral altar, the original focal point, was only gradually overshadowed by the *skene*. The place of performance and the auditorium were spatially continuous and lit by the same sun. Thus, during most of the fifth century, the form of the Greek theatre was an architectural evocation of the function of drama in Greek society. The performance evolved in the midst of its public, just as the drama itself evolved out of society as a manifestation of the public will, a corporate act. The actors were hardly specialist professionals in the modern sense. Although they had mastered a special craft, they were still members of the general public, with wider duties and allegiances. They could not make a full-time living from acting, for there was, as yet, no opportunity (for further discussion see Chapter Two). For most of the year they had to turn to other work. It is appropriate here to recall that when Aeschylus died, his epitaph listed the battles in which he had fought but made no mention of his plays. There was as yet no conception of the theatre as an all-absorbing profession, with the participants sharply distinguished from the spectators. This is best signified by the nature of the chorus, for a long time the most important element in the drama, and drawn from the public at large. The average citizen might have been a spectator one year and a participant the next.

Such a theatre produces active spectators. There is one vital difference between the Greek conception of theatre-in-the-round and ours. In the Greek situation, the audience was totally visible. Modern directors rediscovering the open stage usually, either from necessity or choice, retain the demarcation between performer and spectator which modern lighting techniques provide and to which the proscenium stage has accustomed us. The acting area is illuminated, but not the auditorium. This is hazardous, for the illumination can rarely be completely selective. The front rows on each side come into the spill of the lights and distract the spectators opposite—distract them, be it noticed, only because the use of lighting creates a presumption that the audience is not to be seen. When it *is* seen, therefore, its presence is doubly noticeable.

In the Greek theatre no such convention existed. The players could see the audience and, more important, the audience could see itself. It was conscious of its own presence. Thus we see operating in the theatre the same factors that governed the conduct of public worship or the workings of Athenian democracy. The Greek concept of worship was not that of an active priest preaching to a passive multitude, nor was democratic government interpreted as meaning the handing down of edicts from the governing body (albeit popularly elected) to the governed. In both activities the entire public was spiritedly involved. Nor did the Greek theatrical concept envisage a passive audience. In all three spheres—less distinct, in any case, than in our world—the public was an active partner, free to comment, assist, and intervene. The very form of the theatre was reminiscent of the places of public assembly and induced the same responses. We observe, in consequence, that many Greek plays are little more than staged debates, with the audience hearing each side in turn as the Athenian audience was accustomed to listen to rival orators on the Pnyx, across the valley from the theatre, where the assembly met. In Aristophanes' *The Knights,* a comedy constructed on the lines of a public meeting, to take the most prominent example, the atmosphere of the *ekklesia* (public assembly) colors the entire play, and the identification is almost total. The action is explicitly located in the Pnyx from at least v. 754, but in spirit we might as well be there for the play's entirety.

Theatre and forum, play and debate, are thus, in Greek eyes, architectural and spiritual kin, and the audience can be appealed to directly in the theatre just as it can in the court of law. This is most obvious in comedy, where specific members of the audience are identified by name and where the whole chorus, at certain moments in the play, can turn to the audience and deliver a harangue on current affairs. In tragedy, the scholiasts denote specific lines as intended to be directed at the audience. Such involvement could be positive or negative in value, for the spectators could riposte. We see the negative side in the stories of hostile reactions to offensive characters or sentiments. A familiar means of showing disapproval was to drum the heels; when the audience still sat on wooden benches, the effect must have been formidable, and it is as well to recall here that the superb acoustics of the Greek theatre worked both ways. Aeschylus was pelted with stones in the theatre for divulging, as he claimed inadvertently, secrets of a powerful religious order in one of his plays. There are several stories of the halting of Euripides' tragedies by an infuriated audience.

The positive side is seen most effectively in Aeschylus' *The Eumenides*, the last play in the *Oresteia* trilogy. Here audience participation is progressive, cumulative, and, by the end of the drama, total. The play is opened by Apollo's priestess, the Pythia, who delivers the Prologue identifying the scene as Delphi, her deity's most notable oracular shrine. Aeschylus reminds his audience of sites which must have been familiar from their own visits:

> And in my invocation she that lodges
> In the forecourt of our shrine, Athena, has high place
> And with her I must rank the nymphs in honor,
> Who have their homes in Corycus, the cave
> Where birds find welcome, and the spirits walk.

And Bacchus too—for I am not unmindful—
Has made his home among us . . .

[vv. 23 ff.]*

By subtle reminders of place and association the audience is drawn within the Delphic orbit. By the end of the speech, the imaginative identification is so complete that the theatre has become the shrine and the audience, by implication, visitors to that shrine. Thus, when the Pythia concludes:

If there are Greeks here, let them now draw lots
And enter, according to the custom; and I
Shall give them counsel as the god inspires me

[vv. 37 ff.]

there is no need to imagine, with the more prosaic editors, a stage crowd. She is speaking, simply and directly, to the actual crowd, the audience, whose visible presence surrounds her. They have been drawn within the compass of the play. They have become a character.

In the ensuing episodes, when the action shifts from Delphi to Athens, the audience takes on a new significance. The plot assumes the presence of the Athenian people summoned to watch the trial of Orestes conducted by their patroness deity. Actuality places the Athenian people in the audience. Thus, when Athena addresses the Athenians, the distinction between fact and fiction, allegory and actuality, is imperceptible. We are reminded of Herodotus' story of how the tyrant Peisistratos had himself conducted into Athens by a woman impersonating Athena; and we know why Greek moralists from Solon to Plato regarded the theatre as a potential danger to the commonwealth. The immediacy of the dramatic situation that Aeschylus creates is increased by the contiguity of the theatre and the legendary setting of Orestes' trial. The Hill of the Areopagus, where Aeschylus locates the action, is just round the corner from where his theatre audience is sitting.

The audience, then, has been successively identified, first as

* Verse citations throughout refer to the Greek text.

Greeks in general, and then as Athenians observing a trial set in their remote mythic history. It remains for the concept to become timeless and for past and present to merge as fact and fiction have already done. This is achieved at the end of *The Eumenides* by the simplest means. With the arguments over, Orestes pardoned, and the Furies reconciled to their new status as benefactors of Athens, dramatic time is forgotten. We are brought sharply into the present by the procession of the women of Athens, in which the audience is intended to recognize its own familiar festival, the quadrennial Panathenaia. This procession also permits the playwright to fulfill the basic and most prosaic requirement of his theatre: he ends cleanly and requests applause. The double procession of Furies and Athenian women files out with grandeur:

> Go on your homeward way
> In reverence exalted,
> Children of Night grown old.
> Jocund in processional.
>
> Let all around keep dignity of silence.
>
> To a dwelling old as time
> In the earth's enfoldment,
> In honors proud
> And sacrifices and fair fortune.
>
> Let all around keep dignity of silence.
>
> Visit our land, grave powers.
> With grace and loving kindness.
> Let fire feed on the torches
> And make glad your coming,
>
> Now to our song make acclamation.
>
> There shall be peace for ever
> For Athena's people.
> So has destiny agreed
> And Zeus all-provident.
>
> Now to our song make acclamation.

This concluding refrain is designedly ambiguous. The song referred to is both the women's song that ends the play and the poet's song that is the play itself. The fictional Athenian public is asked for its approbation, and the actual for its applause—in the same breath, for the two are now one. No playwright in his senses would have reversed these invocations and concluded with the appeal for silence. The action has spilled over from the *orchestra* to the auditorium to embrace the whole community, players and public alike, in the same burst of self-glorification; and it is the form of the theatre that makes this communion of spirit possible.

Audience participation on this level was one of the Greek theatre's most vital characteristics. Other examples are manifest both in tragedy and comedy. When Eteocles, in *Seven Against Thebes*, makes his opening address to the citizen body cowering before the threatened assault, he is surely addressing the audience, identified for the moment with the people of Thebes. The same may be true of the Prologue to *Oedipus the King*. Modern directors customarily open the play with the entrance of a stage crowd, composed of the types later specified by the Priest in his appeal to Oedipus—old men, young men, priests, and children. It has recently been argued, however, that such a device is unparalleled in any other Greek tragedy and is particularly strange for Sophocles, who, of all the tragedians, is the most sparing in his use of spectacular crowd effects: elsewhere he seems to go out of his way to avoid them. But, given the design of the Greek theatre, such a crowd would not be necessary. We need to see only Oedipus and the Priest, for wherever the latter stood in the theatre, he would be backed by a sea of faces. If the play was indeed first performed, as most scholars believe, in 429 B.C., when Athens had just passed through a plague as devastating as the Theban epidemic that the Priest describes, the identification of the audience with the play would be cruelly strong.

In comedy, we may consider one powerful moment in Aristophanes' *Thesmophoriazousai* (*Ladies' Day*). The action is located in the annual women's festival of the Thesmophoria, and we are given a taste of the rituals and speeches that would have graced the actual occasion. The presence of the audience reinforces the impression of a large and important concourse. When the Lady Herald makes her proclamation (vv. 295 ff.) she is surely speaking not merely to the chorus but to the theatre at large. We must remember to put the play into its festival context. Such announcements and proclamations were a regular part of the day's activities. Aristophanes takes advantage of this fact to merge the dramatic and the actual to a point where they are virtually indistinguishable. The action once again takes place in the Pnyx, the place of public assembly; and when the women hear that there is a man hiding among them, they announce (vv. 656 ff.): "We must . . . look to see if any other man has slipped through; we must overrun the Pnyx and hunt through all the tents and alleys" (*tas skenas kai tas diodous*). While *skenas* and *diodous* are intelligible here in their nontechnical use, as referring to the tents which the women may be presumed to have erected for their festival encampment, it is difficult to escape the association of words. It seems likely that when the chorus said *skenas*, the audience was reminded of the *skene* (scene-house), and associated the *diodoi* with the gangways in the auditorium. And surely we can imagine the chorus at this point turning on the audience and threatening to search *them*.

There is a similar moment in Aristophanes' *The Clouds*. Strepsiades has had, so he thinks, his son successfully educated in the sophistic school and believes all will go well for him now: he has a home-grown advocate and an answer for anything. He defies his creditors and the world at large. Reaching the height of his dementia, he offers to take on everybody.

> *Oh you poor stupid devils, sitting there*
> *Like stones, just waiting for us clever boys*
> *To work you over, ciphers, sheep, you heap*
> *Of empty vessels!*
> [vv. 1201 ff.]

Here he is surely strutting around the audience and offering to take on any man in the house. By embracing the whole audience in his challenge, he demonstrates the immensity of his conceit.

Acting Areas: The Chorus and Actors

Moving from the auditorium to the performance space, we find a simple but flexible structure offering a variety of acting areas. For the most part the chorus confined itself to the *orchestra*, where unison movement could be most effectively displayed. The chorus, which probably numbered fifty when Aeschylus began to write, was reduced to fifteen by the time Euripides died. Economic factors must have prompted this reduction. The chorus, though unpaid, had to be professionally trained and costumed. This was the financial responsibility of one of the richer citizens, imposed on him as a *liturgy*, or form of taxation in kind. The Greeks gave this citizen the title of *choregus;* we might call him "producer" or "angel," though without the commercial connotations of these modern words. He could expect no return except the kudos, or glory, of sponsoring the prizewinning play and the right to erect a triumphal monument, at his own expense; and the outlay for a large chorus was considerable. We have stories of *choregi* who went bankrupt in order to put on an impressive show. The increasing financial stringency of the war years must have made a reduction in numbers desirable. This, together with the concomitant increase in the number of actors, had the effect of shifting the focus from *orchestra* to *skene*. For the greater part of the fifth century, however, the chorus was still the center of attention, and the carefully patterned dances, accompanied by song, were the main feature of the play.

The actors, for the most part, worked close to the *skene*. Even in the early fifth century, there was probably a raised stage in front of the scenic facade to set them apart and give them necessary prominence. It must be admitted that the existence of such a stage in the early period is one of the most controversial issues in theatrical studies, because archaeological evidence is completely lacking—inevitably, if the early structures were built of wood. However, the literary evidence, though most of it is late, accepts the existence of such a stage from the beginning, and no conclusive arguments have been raised against it. There is no question at this point of a high platform, completely separating the actors from the *orchestra*. That was to come later. We are talking here of a stage perhaps no more than four feet high (the post-holes in the theatres of Corinth and Oropos permit such a reconstruction) with ramps or steps giving easy access to the *orchestra*. There was no reason why actors should not descend to *orchestra* level when necessary. In *Agamemnon*, for example, the length of the choral passage introducing the entrance of the king's chariot suggests that he may have come down the *parodos*, made the circuit of the *orchestra*, and halted by the stage. Clytemnestra then enters at stage level to address him and the chorus. Conversely, there was no reason why the chorus could not be permitted to break formation and mount the platform when necessary. Aeschylus' *The Suppliant Women* and *Seven Against Thebes* indicate such movement. In the former there is a clear distinction between a "high place," a "point of vantage," where the chorus seek sanctuary by the altar of the gods, and the "level ground," to which the King of Argos dismisses them. The action in *Seven Against Thebes* is probably parallel. Here the members of the chorus fall before the divine statues and invoke them by name. Eteocles enters, finds them prostrate, chides them, and persuades them to leave the images. After an interval of twenty lines they begin their next song, presumably in the *orchestra*. Both *The Madness of Heracles* and *Lysistrata* have choruses of old men, who complain of the hill they have to climb. We may imagine them as moving laboriously from the *orchestra* up the steps to the stage, a conventional representation of a steep ascent.

The upper story of the *skene* provided a third acting area. Aeschylus prefers to use it as a conventional "heaven," where supernatural beings may appear. It is on this level that the flying sea-nymphs of *Prometheus Bound* make their first appearance, later descending, as the text indicates, to a more orthodox position in the *orchestra*. Many of the theophanies of Greek tragedy may be located on this *theologeion* ("gods' platform"), that of Athena in *Eumenides*, of Athena in *Ajax*, and Heracles in *Philoctetes*. Euripides sometimes uses the *theologeion* for more prosaic purposes. In the final scene of Aristophanes' *The Clouds*, the upper level represents the roof of Socrates' academy, over which Strepsiades and his slaves swarm in order to set the house on fire. Euripides' *Orestes*, at least in the original version, follows comic example, showing a gibbering slave leaping from the roof of the palace to escape from the horrors within. In *The Phoenician Women* Antigone and the Old Man watch the armies from the roof, and in *The Suppliant Women* the upper level becomes a tower from which Evadne leaps to her destruction—presumably dropping out of sight of the audience behind a low wall or balustrade, evidence for which is preserved in the records of the Theatre of Delos.

Scenic Features and Mechanical Devices

There were certain other permanent scenic features. The *skene* had, of course, a door or doors for entrances. It has been argued that no fifth-century play that we have requires more than one door. There may have been more; the later theatre certainly had three. There is also strong reason to believe that, on the stage in front of the central door, stood a permanent scenic altar, as distinct from the cult altar in the center of the *orchestra*. We may imagine a simple fixture that could be used when required by the action—for Jocasta's prayer to Apollo, for instance, in *Oedipus the King*—and ignored when not; anonymous enough, also, to stand for other objects in special cases, such as the tomb of Agamemnon in *The Libation Bearers* or of the late Pharaoh in *Helen*, and perhaps for the rocky projection on which Oedipus first sits in *Oedipus at Colonos*. In addition, the theatre probably owned a set of statues to dress the stage when necessary. *Seven Against Thebes* requires eight statues of the major deities, and Aeschylus' *The Suppliant Women* at least four. In *Hippolytus* we need to see the images of Artemis and Aphrodite. Apart from this, stage furnishings or large properties were minimal. A few tragedies, like *Alcestis*, require a bier. Conspicuously lacking are chairs and thrones; characters in Greek tragedy rarely seem to sit down, though stools are indicated in the more naturalistic action of comedy, where they are carried on and off by the characters as required.

Mechanical apparatus, too, was rudimentary—from choice, not from necessity, for the Greeks enjoyed a highly developed technology. We can be sure of only two mechanical devices used in the fifth-century theatre. One was a small wagon stage, or wheeled platform (*ekkyklema*, literally "something which can be rolled out"). This could be pushed into sight through the *skene* doors to display significant tableaux, usually scenes of death. The bodies of Agamemnon and Cassandra are thus revealed in *Agamemnon*, as are those of Clytemnestra and Aegisthus in *The Libation Bearers*, its sequel. So, almost certainly, was the corpse of Ajax after his suicide in Sophocles' play of that name. One of the most elaborate tableaux occurs in *The Madness of Heracles*, where we are shown the hero recumbent amid the bodies of the wife and children he has just slaughtered.

The other device was the *mechane*, whose Greek name means simply "machine." This was a crane or derrick to swing characters onto the stage in simulated flight. It seems not to have come into full use until the later fifth century, when the theatre was, in many ways, following a more illusionistic trend. Aristophanes, who burlesques it plentifully, always treats it as a Euripidean, and not simply as a tragic, device, and all the certain examples of its use come from that spectacle-loving dramatist. Bellerophon flew in on the winged horse Pegasus in the lost *Bellerophon* and *Sthenoboia;* Iris and Lyssa descend from the skies in a chariot in *The Madness of Heracles*, as do Castor and Polydeuces in *Electra;* Thetis makes a similar entrance in *Andromache*. The machine seems to have had a maximum load of two characters plus chariot and to have been cumbersome to operate: its appearance is always accompanied by several lines of dialogue to give the characters time to descend to earth, or perhaps to cover the noise. We do not know exactly how it worked or where it was located in the theatre. We do know that actors were fastened to it by a sort of parachute harness, and also that they did not enjoy the experience. A fragment of Aristophanes' *Daidalos* shows a panic-stricken actor swinging from the *mechane* and yelling to the *mechanopoios,* or crane operator, to give due warning when it is about to drop.

The Presentational Theatre

This was the total of the stage equipment. For the most part, any sort of illusionistic spectacle was foreign to the spirit of the fifth-century theatre. We are talking here of a type of performance now usually labeled "presentational." There have been other epithets in the past—"conventional" and "formal" are two—but this is as good as any. It implies, simply, a theatre in which no attempt is made to represent actuality, or to convince the spectators that they are watching "real" people performing a "real" action in a "real" place. Though they may become passionately involved with the argument of a play, they are reminded constantly, by various devices, that they are watching a play and not actuality, art, not life. The one thing that is clear about the Greek theatre at its prime is that its practitioners used no illusionistic scenery, no painted screens or backdrops, to represent Philoctetes' island, Prometheus' mountain top or Agamemnon's palace. There is some evidence that the *skene* was decorated, under Aeschylus or Sophocles, with an architectural design using the newly discovered techniques of false perspective, but this was still decoration merely, like the gnarled pine tree which forms the universal background to the Japanese Nō play, and in no way "scene-painting" in our sense of the word. The *skene* merely provided a formal background against which the actors could perform. It was not intended to depict any specific place. Ubiquitous and unchanging, it set off the action without confining it.

All presentational theatres, of whatever nationality or period, have certain factors in common. One is the frank communion between audience and player that we have already discussed; it is the representational picture-frame stage that pretends that the audience is not there. Another is the way that the setting is suggested to the imagination, either by the playwright's words alone, or by the significance given to permanent architectural elements of the theatre. And the setting is suggested only as specifically as it needs to be. Here we may compare the theatre of Shakespeare, the Elizabethan public playhouse, which operated along the same lines, and about whose workings we know rather more. Often the setting is neutral. In *Macbeth*, it makes no difference to the action where Ross and the Old Man hold their brief dialogue about the storm, so Shakespeare does not bother to tell us. We see the same technique in Aeschylus' *The Persians*, where the setting is at first quite neutral. It is not until the latter part of the play, when the action requires it, that we move in imagination to a place more precisely defined as the tomb of Darius. Where does the action of *Antigone* take place? In Thebes, certainly; and the city is plentifully referred to. But are we supposed to be in the palace or outside it, the *agora*, the council-chamber? We are never told, for it does not matter; dramatic economy is another of the characteristics of presentational theatre.

When environment conditions action, however, the playwright can take all the time he needs to describe it. At the opening of *Prometheus Bound*, we have a brief but evocative word-picture of the desolate heights on which the Titan must be confined. Vase paintings indicate that the rock to which Prometheus is bound was suggested simply by a post or column. Odysseus opens *Philoctetes* with a detailed description of the barren island of Lemnos. There is a cave with entrances from opposite directions, and "a spring below on the left-hand side." Here the necessary physical locations are provided by the permanent features of the stage architecture, and the words apply the local color. The *skene* door stands for Philoctetes' cave, and, probably, the raised stage for the shelf of rock on which it is located; Odysseus and Neoptolemos may well enter at *orchestra* level, for the latter is given a clear direction to "climb" to find the cave.

The *skene* can, in short, stand for any specific building that the play requires—Medea's house in Corinth, the palace of Oedipus at Thebes, or the prophetic shrine of Apollo at Delphi—and the identification is easily accepted by the audience once the *skene* has been appropriately labeled by the opening speakers. Or the same doors can stand for less imposing structures: the shacks in-habited by the Trojan prisoners amid the wreckage of Troy, or the cave of Polyphemos in Sicily. The permanent stage altar, as we have seen, can stand for any specific altar required by the action, for a tomb, or for some natural feature. It is important only to remember that the actual background did not change, except in the mind's eye. Euripides' *Andromeda*, which is set on a rocky promontory, and his *Alcestis*, which requires the cozily domestic environment of Admetus' palace, used identical scenic units. The only difference was in the use that the dramatist made of them and the imaginative picture that he spun around them.

In such a theatre, verbal suggestion can instantaneously create a setting out of nothing. It can as easily erase it. One of the most valuable characteristics of the presentational stage is its flexibility. Neither is the acting area confined by scenery, nor the flow of the action impeded by the necessity for changes. One scene can flow into another without pause, and a supposed change of location requires only the appropriate verbal reference. Thus Shake-speare's neutral, undefined stage could embrace the complex ge-ography of *Antony and Cleopatra* and *Pericles, Prince of Tyre* with ease; and in the same way, the Greek theatre could assume at will a virtually cinematic fluidity without benefit of the camera. This is most obvious in the rapid pace of comedy. Aristophanes' *The Clouds* shifts rapidly between the house of Strepsiades and Socrates' Academy. His *The Peace* begins in Trygaeus' farmyard on earth, moves to Heaven, and then comes down to earth again. The action of *The Frogs*, scenically Aristophanes' most complex play, can easily be adapted to the theatre's basic units. The play begins before the house of Heracles, represented by the *skene* door. Dionysos and Xanthias are then required to cross the River Styx. This is indicated quite simply by having Charon enter in his boat, which may either be drawn on by stage hands or carried on by Charon himself, as in the well-known convention of the Japa-nese Nō play. When the travelers are assumed to reach the other side, the boat is removed, and the *skene* door becomes the tavern from which the Landlady and Plathane enter to assault them. In the next episode, the same door becomes the gate of Hades at which Dionysos knocks to find the fearsome Aeacus with his whip.

But this flexibility is not confined to comedy. It should hardly be necessary to say that the "unity of place" attributed to Greek tragedy by neoclassical theorists is a total fiction. Insofar as it exists at all in the ancient theatre, it is Roman in spirit, not Greek; it is the parallel in dramaturgy to the Roman regularization of theatrical architecture. It is, of course, true that the action of some Greek plays never moves from the environment initially established. *Prometheus Bound, Antigone, Medea,* and *The Bacchae* are cases in point. But in other dramas the scene is supposed to shift, in some cases violently. *The Women of Etna,* a lost tragedy by Aeschylus, had five episodes, each set in a different Sicilian city. In *The Eumenides,* the action begins at Apollo's shrine at Delphi, with the location established by the Pythia's descriptive prologue. In the second part of the play, the action moves with appropriate indications to Athens. Orestes is instructed by Apollo to leave his shrine and make the journey to Athens, there to embrace the statue of Athena. He departs, followed by the chorus of Furies. When he reappears to address the statue, we know that the location is assumed to have shifted; the Furies reinforce this, on their reappearance, by their complaints about their long pursuit. Perhaps the chorus leaves by one *parodos* and returns by another.

A less violent shift occurs in Sophocles' *Ajax,* where we begin outside the tent of Ajax (the *skene* door) and then move to the lonely spot on the seashore. As in *The Eumenides,* the shift is indicated by the exit and reentrance of principal and chorus. When they reappear, the place is supposed to have changed. *The Libation Bearers* also involves a minor shift, from the tomb of Agamemnon to the gates at the palace. The action begins at the tomb, probably the stage altar, and is given a specific identification by Orestes' Prologue:

> Hermes, spirit of the underworld
> And father's regent, lend to me

Your strength, and stand my champion, I pray,
For I am come home to my land again,
And on this mounded tomb invoke my father
To listen and attend.

He is then interrupted by Electra and the chorus, who have come to pour their libations to the dead. Brother and sister recognize each other and join in a prayer for vengeance. Orestes announces his plan of entering the palace in disguise and temporarily withdraws with his friend Pylades. The chorus cover their absence with a song. When Orestes reappears, the scene must be assumed to have shifted to the palace gates, represented by the *skene* doors. The altar-tomb, though still visible, is no longer mentioned, and so, by convention, has ceased to exist. It is referred to only once more during the play, when Orestes and Pylades have won access to the palace, and the chorus nervously await the outcome:

Come friends and fellow-servants all,
Is it not time for us to show
The power of our voices, and so aid
Orestes? O sovereign earth, and sovereign
Mound of the tomb that lie heavy on
The body of the sea-lord and our king,
Now hear us, grant us aid.

[vv. 764 ff.]

Here the altar-tomb, reidentified as such, assumes its former prominence for the moment. Aeschylus has performed a cinematic feat, allowing for the return in a brief flashback to the location of the earlier episodes.

The bare neutrality of the stage creates a scenic ambiguity which the dramatists often find convenient. In the Athenian section of *The Eumenides*, for example, where precisely are we intended to be? A literal interpretation would insist that, when Orestes reappears to embrace Athena's statue, we are on the Acropolis, in the Parthenon, for this is where the image was kept. But the trial of Orestes which follows is specifically identified with the first meeting of the court of the Areopagus; and this was located on another hill adjacent to the Acropolis. But Aeschylus can allow us to move from one to the other without strain. Another example occurs in Euripides' *Hecuba*. Here the action takes place around the Hellespont, the narrow strip of water separating East from West, with Troy on one side and Thrace on the other. But on which side of the water are we intended to be? From the comings and goings of the Greek soldiery, and the frequent references to Achilles' tomb, we should infer that we are on the Trojan side, for that is where the hero was buried, and contrary winds have prevented the army from leaving. But the ghost of Polydorus, Hecuba's murdered son, who speaks the Prologue, specifically identifies the scene as Thrace; and that is where we seem to be in the second half of the play too, when the Thracian king Polymestor receives his dreadful punishment. Euripides uses the scenic ambiguity to assist his manipulation of the double plot. We are on whichever side of the water the exigencies of the immediate dramatic situation require. There is no painted backdrop to stipulate either Troy or Thrace.

The imaginary setting, then, can re-create itself episode by episode, or even moment by moment, depending on what the dramatist requires. A setting created almost entirely in words has no confining force, and need exist only as long as it is convenient. Sophocles' *Oedipus at Colonos*, for example, opens with a detailed description of the supposed place of action. It is the Grove of the Eumenides near Athens, sacred ground, where no man is permitted to set foot. Oedipus and Antigone have trespassed on the precinct unwittingly: they are reproved for this by the chorus and persuaded to move. But there is no subsequent mention of this forbidden territory. The dramatic point has been made, and it is obviously inconvenient to have any part of the acting area on which the actors are prohibited from moving. In the same way, the poet can conjure up pictures of cataclysms and natural disasters. In both *The Madness of Heracles* and *The Bacchae*, Euripides' chorus sings of an earthquake which shakes the palace and sends columns toppling to the ground. As with Prospero's tempest or Lear's storm, no stage mechanics are necessary: it is all in the words. Consequently, there is no need to insist that the effects of the earthquake remain in force, once the relevant scene has passed. Characters who enter subsequently do not comment on the shambles, as we would expect them to do if the scene had been realistically depicted. As always dramatic economy is the keynote.

It follows, then, that we should not pry too literally into matters of place in Greek tragedy. Critics who have attempted this have only brought disaster on themselves. Inconsistencies—or what would be inconsistencies by realistic standards—are apparent. In *Medea*, the Nurse and Tutor are talking anxiously about the dangers that surround Medea's children. At this moment the voice of Medea is heard from inside her house, threatening to kill them. Almost in the same breath, the Nurse tells the Tutor to "keep them away from their mother as much as possible" and to "take them indoors." But this is ludicrous in any literal interpretation, for indoors is exactly where Medea is supposed to be. But the literal interpretation is not what we need here. All the Nurse is saying is "take them offstage before Medea enters." The imaginary setting has been ousted by the technical terminology of the theatre.

Sophocles' *Philoctetes* is an excellent example of the way in which the imaginary setting can adjust itself to the mood of the immediate moment. Apart from the cave-mouth, the island of Lemnos as visualized by Sophocles has no precise topography. The spring identified by Odysseus in the Prologue does not appear to exist for Philoctetes, who talks of his long, painful journeys to find water, or indeed for the chorus, who sing of him "lapping water from any puddle he can find." This stage Lemnos changes subtly according to the speaker. It is a tolerable place of confinement as seen through Odysseus' eyes, a blasted rock according to Philoctetes. When the castaway is in one of his happier moods, he talks of natural features which seem to vanish when he is melancholy. His final invocation to the "nymphs of the streams and meadows," spoken when he knows his imprisonment to be at an end, comes as a considerable surprise after the descriptions we have heard from his lips earlier in the play. The setting constantly re-creates itself according to need.

By the same token, we must be wary of ascribing too literal a function to the stage machinery. Even the scholiasts make this error when they describe the *ekkyklema* (wagon-stage) as showing "things that have happened inside the house." In a sense, it does: in *The Madness of Heracles* the slaughter of the hero's wife and children, which has taken place in the palace, is shown to the audience by means of the wagon-stage. But once the tableau is in place, all sense of "inside" and "outside" is lost, as the language of the scene makes clear. Amphitryon, looking in terror on his sleeping son, cries that he will hide from him, "inside the palace." But if the *ekkyklema* literally represents "inside," Amphitryon's remark is nonsensical: he wants to put as much distance between himself and Heracles as possible. It is clear that the *ekkyklema*'s true function is to bring into prominence important tableaux that have to be pre-set; it does by mechanical means what the modern theatre achieves by lighting.

We may regard the theatre of the fifth century, then, as a magic circle within which the imagination was allowed to work at will. As the years passed, the structure became more substantial by stages whose precise dates must remain indeterminate. The *skene* grew more solid and sprouted wings, *paraskenia*, which enclosed the ends of the stage. In the auditorium, wood was replaced by stone, with seats of honor making up the front tier; in Athens the priest of Dionysos, whose festival this was, sat at the center. In time the whole theatre was to be built of stone, with substantial buildings adjoining it; Pericles had already added an *odeion* (music hall), where meetings associated with the theatre were held and dramatists announced the titles of their forthcoming productions. It was only toward the end of the fifth century, however, that the growing solidity of the theatre was to impinge on the imagination of the dramatist.

CHAPTER TWO

◻

The
Greek Actor

On the art of Greek acting we have even less direct information than on the stage setting. All knowledge of the unique and intricate relationship between music, dance, and the spoken word has vanished. We must constantly remind ourselves that the Greek plays as we possess them are, in effect, libretti for operas whose music we happen to have lost. For large portions of the plays were sung. This was true not only of the choral lyrics (*stasima*) which punctuate the episodes but also of sections of the actors' parts. At moments of high emotional intensity the actor would burst into song. It is rare, nowadays, to see any performance of

Greek drama which attempts even to approximate this musical quality.

Given this loss, however, which immediately removes one dimension of the performance from our understanding, it is still possible to venture certain general statements about the way in which the actor was trained, the qualities which he and his audiences considered admirable, and the factors which governed his playing of the roles. We must speak in the masculine throughout for there were no women in the Greek theatre. Female roles were played by men, and *Lysistrata* and *The Trojan Women* were written for all-male casts. This convention undoubtedly influenced the writers. The women of Greek tragedy tend to be masculine, dominating figures, like Clytemnestra, Hecuba, and Antigone. The gentler, more feminine type, like Ismene, Polyxena, and Deianeira, is less central to the drama.

The Importance of the Actor

In the early period, the actor hardly existed as a distinct figure. It was a poet's theatre, in which the playwright was his own director, composer, choreographer, and leading player. This was still true in the time of Aeschylus, and gave the performance an artistic unity which the theatre scarcely recaptured until the time of Wagner: all aspects of the production were the product of a single creative mind. This monopoly, however, soon began to break down. Aeschylus introduced a second actor, to create more complexity in plays which, before him, had been little more than dramatic oratorios with chorus and a single soloist. Aeschylus' *The Suppliant Women,* though not, as was once believed, our earliest example of Greek tragedy, still preserves this early pattern. To the second actor Sophocles added a third, an innovation which the aging Aeschylus tentatively imitated: the *Oresteia* requires three actors throughout, as does *Prometheus Bound* for its opening scene.

Three remained the standard number. Various reasons have been suggested for this: the aesthetic desirability of self-limitation on the part of the dramatist; economic factors, which prompted the state to control the number of actors it would have to pay; hardening tradition, which made change increasingly difficult; and festival rules, for the playwrights were competing for a prize and it was necessary to ensure that they all started fair, with the same technical means at their disposal. Whatever the reason, all Greek tragedies that we possess can be played with a maximum of three speaking actors. There is one possible exception; *Oedipus at Colonos* seems at one point to need four. It is not difficult, however, to devise simple expedients to circumvent this problem: the parts may have been reshuffled between the three speaking actors and a mute performer, or the lines in question could have been spoken by one of the actors already on stage in another role, while a mute provided the appropriate gestures. As both were masked, the voice would seem to come from the mute. Comedy, in this as in other respects, was less restricted. Several of Aristophanes' plays require four actors.

The limitations on actors, of course, did not limit the number of characters. Each actor could take several parts, and the mask was an aid to versatility. In addition, the dramatist could use as many nonspeaking characters for walk-on roles as the *choregus* was prepared to provide. The limitation simply meant that no more than three speaking characters could appear on stage at the same time. It was necessary for the Greek actor to be a quick-change artist, particularly in comedy. We know from a scholiast's note how long it took to change mask and costume and reappear in a new character. He tells us that Jocasta, who speaks the Prologue in Euripides' *The Phoenician Women,* and Antigone, who enters almost immediately afterward, were played by the same man. He has fifteen lines of verse to make the change, and the short speech by the Tutor which precedes Antigone's entrance is designed to cover the mechanics of this change.

The increasing importance of the actor, counterbalanced by the declining role of the chorus, enhanced his status as an independent artist. This was further improved when the author resigned his part in the performance. Sophocles, we are told, was the first playwright to abandon leading roles to others; his voice was not equal to the strain. He continued to appear in certain parts, particularly when his gymnastic skill could be used, for Sophocles was a notable dancer and was painted on murals in some of the parts he made famous. There is no evidence that Euripides ever acted, and the traditions that Aristophanes played some roles in his own comedies are unreliable, based largely on a misunderstanding of the dramatist's use of the first person singular in his choruses.

The introduction of separate prizes for actors and poets at the Athenian festival of 449 B.C. marked the final divorce of the two functions. Normally the poet continued to direct his own work. There were some exceptions; Aristophanes, who writes feelingly of the difficulties of directing comedy, entrusted several of his plays to others, and Euripides, on at least one occasion, may have done the same. Sophocles' grandson and namesake directed a posthumous production of his grandfather's last play, as well as staging his own.

We may assume, then, for almost all the plays we have, a company as restricted as the theatre's technical equipment. It consisted of the poet, who might also function as actor; a maximum of three actors for tragedy and four for comedy; a chorus; and a variable number of extras. The production staff may have included a choreographer, if the playwright's talents did not extend in this direction: the name of one Telestes, who "invented a number of figures, skillfully miming the dialogue with his hands" is somewhat obscurely linked with that of Aeschylus in this connection, though other sources state firmly that Aeschylus designed his own dances. Dates for Telestes are lacking; he may belong to the pantomime tradition of the later theatre, as a dancer who performed choreographic versions of tragic themes. There were also a mask-maker and a costumer, though original designs were not necessarily prepared for each new play. There were the stage-hands, who worked the machinery, helped with costume changes, and carried furniture when necessary. Aristophanes, who loves to expose the workings of the theatre in order to burlesque them, frequently brings these assistants onto the stage: in *The Birds* and *Lysistrata* the stagehand is called Manes, a slave name. Lastly there were the musicians, who may have worn wooden shoes to keep the beat. The principal instrument was the flute, though there are also references to lyres, trumpets, and various types of percussion effects. Occasionally the actor would have been required to accompany himself, as Sophocles seems to have done on the lyre in his *Thamyras:* in Euripides' *Hypsipyle* the heroine sings to her child accompanying herself on the *krotala,* maracas or castanets.

The Actor's Training

Rehearsals took place in private homes or halls built for that purpose. The choral dances were blocked out with chalk lines on the floor, in a way familiar to anyone who has seen a rehearsal in a TV studio. There is some evidence that the actors learned their parts, not from a script but by a method still familiar in the Mediterranean countries, namely, by hearing the lines read out loud by the author himself or an assistant. We have a description of Euripedes singing lyrics to his chorus in this way. The poet was the teacher (*didaskalos*) of his company, just as he was expected to be the educator of his public.

The actor's concern was chiefly with his voice, the most important part of his professional equipment. In such a theatre this was inevitable. When playing to an audience of fifteen thousand or more, the actor could hope to convey little by visual subtlety. The burden of the drama was carried by the words, and we find ample testimony to this in the surviving plays: the Greek playwright is often forced to use techniques familiar to us from radio drama and to verbalize at length where his modern counterpart could use a stage direction and produce his effect from the actor's facial expression or gestures. In the Greek theatre, the actor could always rely upon being heard. The acoustics were superb, and still are, though the *skene,* which would have acted as as sounding board, is now usually demolished. A favorite tour-guide's trick at

Epidauros is to drop a coin or strike a match in the center of the *orchestra:* the sound can be clearly heard from the rearmost benches. It is sometimes held that the actor's mask contained a built-in megaphone to project the voice. This is merely hypothetical. Later authors report other devices. Actors became adept at bouncing their voices off the wooden panels of the *skene.* Large vessels tuned to resonate to certain pitches of the actor's voice were placed in the auditorium. (This device, described by Vitruvius, was adapted by preachers in the Renaissance.) But the fifth-century actor needed no such aids and relied on his own ability: the aids are a mark of the decadence. It is worth remarking here that, in spite of the excellence of their theatres, the Greeks seem to have been strangely ignorant of, or indifferent to, the minor details of acoustics. Even as late as Vitruvius, it was popularly held that wooden construction was acoustically better than stone, and Aristotle tells how the voices of the chorus were blurred when straw was spread in the *orchestra.*

Ancient critics are unanimous in judging actors by their voices, using terminology we would now apply to opera singers. Aristotle defines acting as being "concerned with the voice, and how it should be adapted to the expression of different emotions." Elsewhere he couples acting and music as similar arts. A dictum attributed to Demosthenes states that "actors should be judged by their voices, politicians by their wisdom." Plato, Zeno, and a number of lesser figures implicitly accept these assumptions. It is interesting to compare modern comments on the theatre to the ancient ones: that of Elmer Rice, for example, who writes, apropos of Gordon Craig, that "he is certainly right in his contention that most people go to the theatre to *see* plays performed"; or that of Stark Young, arguing that "of the two sensuous avenues by which the art of the theatre is apprehended, the eye and the ear, the eye at present is the one we travel most importantly." In this contrast lies the whole difference between the ancient theatre and our own.

The Greek actor trained his voice rigorously. Here again the parallel with the modern opera singer is evident. Aristotle stresses the need for a careful diet if the voice is not to be spoiled. Thus the epithet "roast-meat actor" (*opsophagos*), applied to an actor, was a term of abuse: almost our "ham," though not equivalent. Tonics were taken to improve the voice. There is a case on record of a nondramatic *choregus* who poisoned one of his boy choristers by careless administration of the tonic. The evidence from this trial shows the elaborateness of the training, which was surely the same for the dramatic chorus: no less than four people were appointed to look after the chorus members, and no expense was spared. Stories of the great orators contain other examples of voice-training exercises. Demosthenes, who was trained by an actor, learned clear articulation by speaking with a mouthful of pebbles and delivered speeches on the seashore to accustom himself to the murmur of the assembly. The performers struggled to attain perfection, for they faced a keenly critical audience, exposed in the everyday machinery of the democracy to the finest speakers of their time, and quick to pounce upon a fault. The comic writers record slips of diction which seem inconsiderable to us, but were seized on with derision by the audience and could blemish an actor's reputation for years. In the theatre, actors rehearsed their voices up to the moment of their appearance. The comic actor Hermon once missed an entrance because he was preoccupied with his exercises backstage.

The actor's delivery was marked by a strong rhythmical beat which could easily turn into song. In Greek tragedy, the basic verse pattern was the iambic trimeter, recognized by the ancients as the closest equivalent to the rhythms of everyday speech. The sung passages, both for actors and chorus, used more complex lyric meters. Comedy was more eclectic, and the metrical scheme of a play by Aristophanes varies widely. There are indications that Greek tragedy, at least, abhorred the dramatic pause and that breaks in the musical continuo were employed only for extraordinary effects. We get some impression of continuity from the plays themselves, where all necessary movement and business seem to be covered by dialogue. Nor was there, so far as we can see, any attempt at vocal impersonation. All actors used the same standard form of tragic declamation. The great tragedian Polus, who flourished in the latter half of the fifth century and may have been one of Demosthenes' instructors, used the same grandeur of delivery for king and beggar alike. When we recall that the actors were also wearing masks, the problems of distinguishing one speaker from another are evident. The dramatists are clearly aware of this difficulty and take great pains—as must a radio dramatist—to let us know who is speaking at any given moment. Nor did tragedy commonly distinguish age, race, or geographical origin by dialect, although references to foreign speech are frequent. In *The Libation Bearers*, for example, Orestes announces that he and Pylades, to gain admittance to the palace, will disguise themselves as travelers; they will "assume the language of Parnassus, and talk the way men do in Phocis." But when they reappear to execute their plan and introduce themselves to Clytemnestra, they are doing no such thing. The text makes it clear that they are still using the standard Attic-Ionic dialect of tragedy. We may compare the familiar convention of film, where characters established as French or German speak perfect English throughout, perhaps with an occasional foreign phrase slipped in for local color. In *The Persians,* Aeschylus uses a deliberately exotic vocabulary which was still comprehensible to a Greek audience. Comedy, of course, was another matter. Closer to the vernacular, it used dialect frequently: Aristophanes' Spartans speak Doric, his Thebans Boeotian, and his Persians a meaningless mumbo-jumbo spiritually akin to the comic French and German of our own popular farces.

Costume and Mask in Tragedy

In costume also there was considerable divergence between tragedy and comedy. In both, the most important element was the mask. For the fifth century at least, the tragic mask was not the distorted grotesque so often shown in illustrations of Greek tragedy. The surviving evidence, though slight, shows it to have been simple and straight-forward, a conventional heightening of the normal human features. The grotesque, horrific mask came at a later period, together with the exaggeratedly padded costume; both stem from Roman misconceptions of what Greek tragedy had been. As for the tragic costumes, these seem to have been at first strictly formal in nature, and no more intended to represent real costumes than the stage setting was meant to depict an actual place. We are told that the costumes designed by Aeschylus for his plays were copied and used as robes by the priests at Eleusis. This gives a valuable clue to their nature; they were probably all-purpose garments that could be worn, with minor alterations, for a variety of characters. Second-hand shops did a good trade in used costumes, and it seems that actors were expected, as in stock companies now, to provide their own basic wardrobe. We are told of Sthenelos, a fifth-century playwright and actor, who was forced to sell his costumes when he fell on evil days.

Tragic costume seems to have employed a simple and obvious color symbolism. Kings wore purple, priests white, and young girls yellow. Death in *Alcestis*—probably a burlesque of a similar character in tragedy—wears black wings and carries a large sword. Color symbolism was also extended to the masks; hair was white for age, and cropped for slaves and characters in mourning. Some characters are specified as "golden-haired"—for example Medea's children and the tyrant Lycus in *The Madness of Heracles*. Foreigners may have been indicated by a richer, more exotic dress: there is some evidence for this in Aeschylus' *The Persians* and also in his *Suppliant Women*, where the chorus are Egyptians. Strabo, the Roman geographer, complains of the tragic poets' tendency to confuse oriental races, and it is tempting to suppose a generalized oriental costume, in the manner of the Elizabethan theatre, which had no precise geographical affinities but merely reproduced the popular idea of Eastern dress.

Necessary indications of rank or function were given by the props that the character carried. Tragic kings, as we know from Aristophanes' parodies and other sources, invariably carried a scepter with an eagle carved on the top. Warriors had double throwing spears, in the Homeric manner. Heralds wore wreaths and travelers, like Hermes in Sophocles' *Inachus* and Ismene in his *Oedipus at Colonos,* a wide-brimmed hat. (This may have been the only "disguise" that Orestes assumed in *The Libation Bearers.*)

There is considerable controversy about what tragic actors wore on their feet. It used to be believed that the tragic boot, *kothurnos,* had elevated platform soles to increase the actor's stature by several inches. The majority of present-day scholars no longer think this to be true and argue instead for a boot with high uppers, that is, one which came high up the leg. It is impossible to be conclusive, as the available evidence can be interpreted either way. As so often in the Greek theatre, the details are obscure but the general impression is clear. The effect of the mask and formal costume was to depersonalize the tragic actor, in the same way that the neutral setting gave a timeless quality to the drama.

Movement and Gesture

For the tragic actor's movement and gestures we have the usual evidence—plays, scholia, vases—with one additional source of some importance, the art of public speaking. In the ancient world, acting and rhetoric were kindred arts. A speech was expected to be rehearsed, moreover, in movement as well as in diction, for the Greek orator used his whole body. We know of several prominent politicians who took instructions from actors, and of actors who entered politics or performed occasional diplomatic missions for the state. Thus we may use the studied gestures of the orator, about which we know rather more, to fill out our scanty knowledge of the actor. The connection endured through Roman times and beyond. Quintilian's treatise on rhetoric, in which he lists and analyzes a number of gestures, looks back to fifth-century Greece and forward to the speaker's manuals of the Renaissance. Though we have no such exhaustive work for the fifth century, we have numerous passing references to the gestures that the orators used, and may parallel these with indications in the plays.

The open-air theatre dictates its own terms: acting must necessarily be broader than indoors; and this was particularly true in the Greek theatre with its vast audience. In addition, the actor was deprived by the mask—as he would have been by the distance alone had he worn no mask—of the play of facial expression, which his modern counterpart finds indispensable. Small movements would have had no meaning, and every gesture had to carry to the furthest seats. We must look, then, for simplicity and exaggeration: for a system of movements unambiguous in meaning and perceptible even to the spectators furthest from the stage. We must look, in fact, for a repertoire of gestures akin in spirit to those of classical ballet. There is evidence of this exaggeration, even in the texts of the plays, in the matter of age. Characters in tragedy are either young, or in the prime of life, or old; and the old are very old indeed. The aged characters verge on the senile. Teiresias needs to be supported, and Hecuba can hardly hold herself upright. There are no subtle gradations of age, and we never, even in the *Oresteia,* see a character growing old. This concept, so far as we may see, applies to Greek acting as a whole. We may isolate and identify certain movements and gestures, each evoking a distinct emotion, and each broad enough to be absolutely clear.

Grief, as one would expect, is one of the most clearly recorded emotions in tragedy. Often a simple verbal indication suffices: the character is described as weeping or turning pale. It should be noted here that the mask, for the benefit of those who are close enough to see, is not rigid. With the help of a willing imagination, it assumes the look that it is said at any given moment to have. Like the neutral scenic facade, it takes on the coloration dictated by the dramatic moment. One is reminded of the famous Russian film experiment in which the same shot—a close-up of a peasant's face—was shown in a variety of contexts. On each occasion, the audience swore that they had seen a different expression. When Medea is described as weeping, or when the slaves in *The Libation Bearers* sing of the blood coursing down their nail-torn cheeks, there would be many in the audience prepared to swear they saw these things. But there were suitable accompanying gestures also. A veil might be thrown over the face. Thus Aeschylus showed the mourning Achilles and Niobe; in Euripides' *Electra,*

Orestes asks his sister why she weeps, muffling her head. Another gesture was to drop the head and look at the ground. Creon so describes Antigone at her time of grief. Vase paintings which show this attitude—and there are many—customarily show the hands supporting the head, or raised to the forehead in the conventional gesture of melancholy.

Mourning, though a part of grief, has a gesture-language of its own, deriving from actual mourning ritual. Well into historical times this was extremely violent (as Greek funerals still tend to be) to the point of self-mutilation. The hair and garments were torn, and the cheeks bloodied with the nails. Solon, the sixth-century lawgiver, prohibited these excesses, but the gestures survived in stylized form in tragedy. Thus the opening chorus of *The Libation Bearers:*

> *Forth from the palace gates, as I was bid,*
> *With urns I come, with drumming hands,*
> *Torn cheeks, the nail's fresh furrow*
> *A talisman of red*
> *And in my heart old sorrow,*
> *With rending of my robes, with fingers*
> *Wild from the tearing at my breast*
> *In grief of glad days gone.*
>
> [vv. 23 ff.]

Here the old gestures are transformed by the stylization of dance, just as the beating of the breast which accompanies *mea culpa* in the Catholic liturgy is a vestigial memory of actual penances.

The attitude of supplication, perhaps the most familiar of ancient gestures, is noted frequently in the plays. The suppliant kneels at his interlocutor's feet, throws one arm around his knees, and with the other hand grasps his chin or beard. (This is what the frequent "I beg you by your beard," puzzling to the uninitiated, means in Greek tragedy.) Thus, in Sophocles' *Oedipus at Colonos,* Antigone and Ismene beseech Polyneices, who struggles to escape. In Euripides' *Andromache*, the heroine is on her knees before Peleus, but her hands are bound and she complains that she cannot touch his face. In the same author's *Hecuba*, the aged queen clasps Agamemnon by the knees and hand.

A few other gestures whose dramatic usage is attested may be listed briefly here. In prayer to the Olympian gods, the arms were outstretched with the hands palm upward. For the chthonic deities, the palms were turned down and the ground struck with the foot. We may imagine Medea thus when she commits herself to the murder of her children:

> *No, by the powers that dwell in Hell below,*
> *It shall never come to this, that I abandon*
> *My sons to be insulted by their enemies.*
> [Euripides, *Medea*, vv. 1059 ff.]

A pirouette, perhaps, could express joy: we know at least that this was an orator's gesture, for Aeschines ascribes it to Demosthenes. The participants in an oath joined hands.

The gestures of the tragic stage were patterned movement on the verge of becoming dance. At moments of heightened emotion they actually did so, just as the actor's iambics melted into song. In Euripides' *The Phoenician Women*, Jocasta, though characterized as weary and slow with age, can still display joy with her whole body in the movements of the dance. In *The Trojan Women*, the chorus can invite the aged Hecuba to show her emotion in the same way. We should remind ourselves again that we are not dealing with illusionistic theatre. There is no more incongruity in having an old weary queen dance than there is in having Doctor Coppelius do so in the ballet.

Dance

Dance, like song, was a vital ingredient of tragedy from the earliest times. Thespis, Phrynichus, Pratinas, and Choerilos, all figures from the early theatre, had a high reputation as dancers. Aeschylus was credited with inventing a number of new figures. There is an obvious parallel here with the Eastern dramatic tradition. In Sanskrit the words for "dance" and "drama" are the same, and in Japan the dance is the kernel of the Nō play. In Greece, the connection continued through the fifth century. Plutarch records the boast of Phrynichus that he invented "as many dance figures as there are waves on the sea." Sophocles himself was an accomplished dancer and led the chorus around the trophy erected to celebrate the Greek victory at Salamis. There is a reference to his "playing ball" in one of his own works which probably implies a separate dance episode inserted into the dramatic context.

Greek dancing was—as it is to a large extent today—highly mimetic. It aimed not so much at providing a rhythmical sequence of abstract patterns as at a direct, often broad, imitation of familiar types and activities from everyday life. Plutarch outlines the system on which it was based: the dance was an *enchaînement* of steps and fixed poses or attitudes (*schemata*), each intended to represent some distinct character, activity, or emotion. His evidence, of course, is late, but the mimetic nature of the Greek dance at all periods is well attested. We have Aristotle's testimony for the fourth century, and Plato's before him. Much later, Lucian relates a graceful compliment to a dancer in the time of Nero: "I not only see, I hear what you are doing; you seem to be talking with your very hands." This is reminiscent of the praise of Aeschylus' dancer, Telestes.

We know of dances representing a wide variety of subjects. Dioscorides mentions an Aristagoras who "danced a Gallus" (a eunuch priest of the goddess Rhea). There was the war dance (*pyrriche*) in full armor, a Cyclops dance, another representing the gait of old men, and a tracking dance (*skops, skopos,* or *skopema*). Out of a bewildering complexity of names—for once, we have too much information—three principal types of dramatic dances emerge. These were the *emmeleia* for tragedy, the *cordax* for comedy, and the *sikinnis* for the satyr play. We know that the *emmeleia* could be a dance for individual performers as well as for a chorus. Pollux also gives us a list of the *schemata*, or poses, of tragic dancing. For most of them, we can only guess at the meaning. "Upturned hand" and "downturned hand" are self-explanatory and perhaps can be identified with the prayer gestures discussed above. *Kalathiskos* may imply holding the hands above the head, as though carrying a basket thereon. *Thermaustris* ("tongs") may mean what we would call the splits. Like *kybistesis* ("somersault"), it suits oddly with a style of dancing testified to be grave and dignified and reinforces the impression that the Greek conception of dancing, or indeed of the gravity of tragedy, was not necessarily our own. Athenaeus, another late commentator, duplicates Pollux' list with some additions. *Xiphismos* ("sword thrust") is particularly interesting; Athenaeus also describes the *skops* as "putting the hand to the forehead, in the manner of one looking out." We may imagine the searching satyrs in Sophocles' *Ichneutai* performing a dance of this nature as they pantomime the hunt for Apollo's cattle. This list also adds the *strobilos,* or pirouette: the three sons of Carcinus, the tragic playwright, were adept at this.

Acting and Costume in Comedy

Comic acting, as we might expect, was of a very different nature. It was, from the beginning, more physical. Aristophanes fell heir to a whole legacy of slapstick "bits," which he plundered and re-ordered much as the early film makers did the accumulated treasure of vaudeville and burlesque. We know from the playwright himself what some of these were: he lists them in a chorus of *The Clouds.*

> So, like Electra in the tragedy,
> Enter my comedy, to see if she can find
> A public as enlightened as the first.
>
> Please mark the fact
> That she's a decent, self-respecting girl. To start with
> There isn't any leather pink-tipped phallus
> Dangling on her costume for the boys to laugh at,
> No jokes about bald heads, no hoochy-coochy dances.

No old men covering the thinness of the dialogue
With slapstick; nor does she come on the scene
With blazing torches, screaming "Save me! Help!"

[vv. 534 ff.]

All the tricks that Aristophanes affects to deride, he uses himself; his plays are full of them, for they were well loved. Another favorite piece of business was to have characters scattering nuts among the audience; yet another, to apply a lighted torch to another actor's behind. This occurs so frequently that it might almost be called the Greek equivalent of the custard pie; in *Ladies' Day*, Aristophanes writes a whole scene around it. The actors were obviously free to improvise stage business. We know that the comic actor Hermon would lay about him with his stick to get an easy laugh. The *cordax*, the traditional comic dance, shared these characteristics. It is described as fast moving and lascivious. Philocleon, the severe old jurist, new come to levity, performs such a high-kicking dance at the end of *The Wasps*.

✓The comic costumes, as we know from surviving illustrations and figurines, more closely approximated everyday clothing. Their basis was a short tunic and tights, which allowed for athletic movement; they could, however, be grotesquely and obscenely padded, as witness the Aristophanic passage quoted above. The masks were grotesque caricatures and often modeled after the actual living Athenians whom Aristophanes burlesqued in his plays. Socrates, in *The Clouds*, is the most notable example: there is a story that the real Socrates stood up in the audience when his caricature waddled on stage to allow the audience to compare them. There is another story that Aristophanes' mask maker refused to make the likeness of Cleon, the vitriolic demagogue and Aristophanes' archenemy, for fear of repercussions. ✓

The Actor and His Role

How did the fifth-century actor approach his part? A story of the late fifth-century tragedian Polus, first told long after his death by Aulus Gellius, is often quoted to prove a high degree of emotional involvement. In playing Electra in Sophocles' tragedy, he is said to have substituted for the property urn carrying the supposed ashes of Orestes those of his dearly loved son, to give authenticity to his grief. But, if true, this story must represent a considerable departure from customary practice. A greater degree of detachment is normal in the presentational theatre, where character is revealed by externals (that is, costume, mask, stage properties, and an accepted code of conventional gestures) rather than by inner motivation. The actor wearing a mask is performing an act different in quality from the actor who disguises his face with greasepaint. The latter is attempting to make you believe that he is really something he is not; the former is admitting that, for the time being, he is pretending to be something that he is not. His assumption of the mask is an open admission of artifice; the audience is left in no doubt that this is still a performance. The Greek actor assumed a character by literally assuming a mask and a costume. To this extent, the mask and costume *are* the character, and the actor merely the mechanism that gives them temporary motion. The same convention operates, for example, in the *commedia dell'arte*. When the player donned the mask and costume of Pantalone, he was not merely putting on a disguise, but was accepting, together with the mask, all the associations of character and traditional behavior that came with it. He was governed by them, not they by him. He was at liberty to improvise and, to an extent, to color the role by his own personality, but only within the limits that the mask and costume imposed on him.

This concern with outward representation as the key to character in Greek drama was evidently felt by the writers. In *Ladies' Day*, Aristophanes caricatures the tragic poet Agathon by showing him dressed in appropriate costume while writing female parts in one of his tragedies. This is not merely a joke about Agathon's effeminacy (though this is also implied): it anticipates by almost a century Aristotle's advice to the poet to adopt the very look and gestures of his characters as an aid to composition. We may substantiate this from pictorial evidence: there are several representations of both poets and actors studying the stock masks and presumably drawing inspiration from them. These suggest the technique still practiced in the classical Japanese theatre, where Nō and kabuki actors preface their performance by a long period of silent contemplation before a mirror. The habit endured well into Roman times: a letter written about A.D. 162 remembers how "the tragedian Aesopus is said never to have put on his tragic mask without placing it before him and studying it for a long time, in order that he might suit his gestures and adapt his voice to the features of the mask."

To what extent may this identification of costume with persona be found in Greek drama, and how far does it infringe on the personality of the individual actor? It may be seen in one conspicuous way in tragedy. There are several scenes in which characters partially divest themselves of their costumes onstage, and this disintegration of the costume is followed by the destruction of the character. Costume and persona are so closely identified that any infringement of the one must be followed by the diminution of the other. Thus Cassandra, standing defeated before the palace of Argos in *Agamemnon,* strips herself of the emblematic features of her costume. She tears off her wreaths and throws down her prophetic staff. The destruction of the emblems of prophecy is followed by the destruction of the prophetess whose nature they symbolize: Cassandra enters the palace to die. Agamemnon, earlier in the same play, removes his shoes before walking on the purple carpet that leads to his death. He has symbolically diminished his stature; this would have even greater effect if the tragic boots did indeed have high platform soles, as used to be believed. In *Hippolytus,* the delirious Phaedra tears off her clothes; so does Hermione at the moment of her desperation in *Andromache.* In *The Madness of Heracles,* Megara and the children of Heracles exchange their garments for shrouds. The significance of costume is here developed by Euripides as usual, in a way peculiarly his own. There is a double reversal. Megara and the children have attired themselves for death but are then apparently saved; Heracles, resurrected, emerges as their deliverer. But the damage has been done, and the change of costume (given additional point here by the funereal associations of the new garb) prepares the audience for the fact that their salvation is illusory. They must die in the end. We may also adduce certain comic parallels, such as the stripping of the old men in *Lysistrata* when they are worsted by the women's chorus, and their reclothing at the moment of reconciliation. The Commissioner is also symbolically stripped after Lysistrata defeats him in debate, when his regalia is taken from him and replaced by burlesque substitutes.

The vital connection between costume and persona is seen most clearly in Old Comedy in the beating of Dionysos and Xanthias, in the last scene of the first half of *The Frogs*. Dionysos has disguised himself as Heracles to facilitate his journey to the underworld. Assaulted by Aeacus, the porter of Hades, he begs Xanthias to take the Heracles costume. Xanthias' impersonation is so fortunately rewarded that Dionysos demands the lionskin back. He is promptly set upon by the Landlady and Plathane and another exchange is effected. Aeacus reappears and is unable to distinguish between them. (It will be noted that the individual personalities of the actors make no difference. The costume makes the character, and whoever wears the lionskin is, for the moment, Heracles.) The impasse is resolved by Xanthias' suggestion that Aeacus should thrash both of them. The real god, being impervious to mortal pain, will not cry out.

Logic demands, therefore, that Dionysos, who is the true god, should not suffer from his beating. In fact, he suffers considerably and, though trying to conceal it, cries as loudly as the mortal Xanthias. There is more here than the arbitrary abandonment of Dionysos' divinity to serve an immediate comic effect. It is as if, in the repeated passing of the costume from one to the other, their characters had somehow been confused and merged. By sharing the same costume, they have come to share certain characteristics.

Or is it simply the actor behind the persona who cries out? Aristophanes, who delights in exposing the mechanics of his theatre, often lets us see the human being behind the mask, a deliberate flouting of the theatrical conventions for comic effect. A notable example appears in *The Acharnians*, where Dikaiopolis, threatened with death by the chorus, seeks to move them by dressing in a tragic beggar costume borrowed from Euripides. In the long speech that follows, we see, first, the actor speaking not as Dikaiopolis but, simply and frankly, as an actor performing the part of Dikaiopolis in a play, admitting that he is in a theatre and that an audience is present; second, as Dikaiopolis himself, disguised as a beggar and pleading for his life; and third, as Dikaiopolis apparently so convinced by his own disguise that he identifies himself with the part he is playing; while the chorus, who have permitted him to adopt the guise in the first place, seem to end by accepting it as fact.

Dikaiopolis first announces (v. 416) "I must speak a long oration to the chorus today, and if I speak badly, it will mean my death." In one breath he reminds the audience that they are, after all, watching a play—he uses the technical terminology, "chorus," and not "Acharnians"—and at the same time reaffirms the dramatic illusion by saying that his life will depend on the kind of speech he makes. We see the same ambiguity when he begins to plead. He apologizes directly to the spectators (v. 496) saying that, although his defense of the Spartans will not please them, it is none the less true. He reminds them again that they are watching a play: "We're by ourselves, and this is the Lenaea; there are no foreigners in the house." The chorus, however, is not perturbed by this deliberate dropping of character. They even forget that it was they who permitted him to adopt the beggar disguise in the first place, and speak as if he were really what he seemed: "you dare to say such things to me—a beggar?" A few lines later, Dikaiopolis is either deceived by his own impersonation or performing it with great enthusiasm. He is confronted by the general Lamachus, furious that a beggar like Dikaiopolis should take such liberties with his tongue, and excuses himself on the grounds of his humble origins: "O Lamachus, hero, please forgive me if, beggar that I am, I spoke out of turn." Shortly afterward, however, he is indignant that the soldier should mistake him for being what he has pretended to be all along:

LAMACHUS: You talk that way to your general—you, a beggar?
DIKAIOPOLIS: What, me, a beggar?
LAM: Well, who are you then?
DIK: Who am I? An honest citizen.

This separation of the actor from his role is of the essence of presentational theatre. Greece had discovered the *Verfremdungseffekt* centuries before Brecht. What appears so blatantly in comedy must also have operated in tragedy, where the actor was debarred from psychological identification with his role by the fact that he was often playing several interlocking parts in the same play. He saw his performance piecemeal. This communicates itself to the writing. In both tragedy and comedy, we often find what now appear as gross inconsistencies of characterization, which give modern actors some trouble. As usual, the most blatant examples are in comedy. Dionysos, in the first half of *The Frogs*, is the consummate intellectual, who knows his Euripides backward. In the second half, confronted with the playwright in person, he cannot understand a word of what his favorite is saying. The change here is dictated by the immediate dramatic circumstances. In the first half, Dionysos is confronted with Heracles, the aesthete with the athlete. Dionysos is the know-all, Heracles the booby. But in the second half, Dionysos presides over the trial between Aeschylus and Euripides. There are, potentially, three clever men on stage. Aristophanes needs a foil for the intellectual duel of the two tragedians and has no compunction in manipulating the character of Dionysos to suit the circumstances. In Aristophanes, the character changes to fit the joke, not the joke to fit the character.

The same is true, though it is less obvious, in tragedy. We see it in the "double-plot" plays of Euripides. Both Medea and Hecuba are virtually two different characters, sufferers in the first half of their tragedies, savages in the second: and though the modern actor may, with difficulty, find some plausible psychological motivation to connect the two, it is doubtful whether the author, or the Greek actor, would have recognized any problem.

Greek characters were normally not considered *in extenso;* they were continually redefined in terms of a cross-section of the play at any given moment, and by the immediate point which the dramatist wished to make. Characterization, like the stage setting, was flexible.

In summary, we may stipulate certain requirements for the fifth-century actor. He had to have a fine voice and be both physically and emotionally versatile. He also required considerable physical stamina, for he was not only an actor but a singer and dancer as well. The mere fact of wearing a mask added considerably to the exhaustion of the performance. Some actors, like Apollogenes, a notable prize fighter, were successful athletes also. It may not be coincidental that Euripides had some reputation in athletics. The same emphasis on physical fitness prevailed through Roman times: Cicero could say that "philosophy is as necessary for the speaker as the gymnasium for the actor." The actor's diet has already been noted. Plato sees these restrictions as a humiliation and suggests—as a milder alternative for the training of competing choruses in his Ideal State—total abstinence for boys under eighteen and only moderate drinking for men under thirty. Modern actors would find this severe enough, but the Greek discipline was rigorous; it was even urged that actors should abstain from sexual relations while developing a part.

But though their indulgences were limited, actors preparing for the festivals were carefully looked after and given any luxury that would not be harmful. The Athenians were accused, by an anonymous Spartan, of spending on the theatre sums sufficient to support a whole army and navy and feeding their troops peasant food while the actors enjoyed the choicest delicatessen. Such pampering was balanced by the exigencies of the performance. Aristotle bears witness to the great thirst of the actor Parmenon when he came offstage. But many flourished under the regime. Polos played eight tragedies in four days at the age of seventy. And it was, in the fifth century at least, a not unrewarding life. The actor's income was limited; he received some payment from the state, though probably not enough to keep him through the year. The prestige gained from festival performances, however, would put him in great demand as a teacher of public speaking, and success in Athens might lead to invitations elsewhere. The fifth-century actor could look forward to a reasonable degree of security and considerable honor.

CHAPTER THREE

The
Theatre in a
Changing
Greece

The preceding chapters have outlined the general features of Greek play production during the theatre's most creative period. By and large, these features remained unchanged throughout the fifth century: the plays of Aeschylus and Euripides differed hardly at all in their technical requirements. Within the overall pattern, however, there was plentiful room for variation, and we may already distinguish in the fifth century the beginnings of certain trends that were to bring about widespread changes in the fourth, and later. We see a gradual transformation from a theatre which was flexible, imaginative, and wholly presentational in its staging methods to one which was more narrowly defined and attempted to give spectators the illusion that they were watching a "slice of life." We see this new concept evolving in acting, costuming, and the employment of the conventional stage setting. And many of the changes are directly attributable to Euripides, an innovator in production as in playwriting.

Euripides' Innovations

Although we know Euripides the man mostly from the adverse comments of his critics, the originality of his stage conception shines through. For him, as for all Greeks, the drama was a teaching medium. Where he differed from his contemporaries was in his notion of what should be taught, and how. He was vitally concerned with the day-to-day problems of his society, and a vicious critic of its flaws. Though still employing the traditional mythic-heroic material, he sought to emphasize in his stories those qualities that were immediately relevant to a fifth-century audience. His intent, as Aristophanes shows in parodic form, was to humanize tragedy; to abandon Aeschylean metaphysics for sophistic pragmatism; to deal with problems which no longer belonged to the rarefied atmosphere of theological speculation, but to the everyday, the here and now; and to force his audience, by reinterpreting the stock situations of myth, to a new evaluation of the stock situations of life. To this end, though bound by the rules and traditions of the dramatic festivals to a system of conventions, which he plainly resented, he sought to ground his characters and plots more firmly in actuality and show his audiences, in effect, things which might as well be happening to them. For his opponents, this was a diminution of the grandeur of tragedy; for Euripides, it was the exploitation of its full potential. He created characters more human than those of Aeschylus and Sophocles had ever been, "warts and all," and revealing the pettiness as well as the dignity of the human condition. The personages of his dramas are no longer drawn chiefly from kings, queens, and supermen, but embrace the lowest levels of society: *Medea,* his earliest extant tragedy, opens typically with a sustained passage of servants' gossip. Into their mouths he put language that, increasingly through his career, broke down the standard rhythms of Greek tragic verse and approximated the vernacular more closely, in both vocabulary and speech patterns. Euripides has been accused of writing barely versified prose. His music, according to Aristophanes, who burlesqued it, was adapted from popular sources. It is a double pity that both the original and the burlesques have vanished.

In production, Euripides sought to give a plausibly naturalistic coloration to inherited conventions that his predecessors had taken for granted. This was essential to his purpose, if he was to convince his audiences that the things he wrote of belonged to their world. We see it most obviously in his handling of the choruses. Clearly the conventions often exasperated him, particularly in the plays of intrigue, which he loved—for how could one justify the constant presence of a group of fifteen people placed where they could hear every word of the plots the principals were making? He could not eliminate them entirely, for the chorus was a condition of the contest. (There is a tempting theory, unfortunately without sufficient evidence, that some of Euripides' plays were originally designed for private performance, where the normal regulations would not apply.) He experiments with the stage aside; in *Hecuba,* at the beginning of the scene between the aged queen and Agamemnon, Hecuba has several lines which the king is supposed not to be able to hear. But he obviously felt that to confer deafness on an entire chorus would have been to carry things too far. Sometimes, then, the chorus is sworn to secrecy. In *Medea,* the women of Corinth are made a party to the plot from the beginning, so that the protagonist may formulate her revenge openly. This solution to a particular problem exemplifies Euripides' attitude to the chorus generally. Its members lose their old objectivity (and with it, much of their contact with the audience); they forfeit their double function as both participant and commentator and become totally involved with the immediate action. The chorus becomes a stage crowd. In *Ion,* its members are characterized virtually as tourists, entering the precincts of the shrine of Delphi and commenting on the marble wonders as tourists are accustomed to do on such occasions. We may contrast this with the way Aeschylus handled the same situation in *The Eumenides* (see p. 18).

In Euripides' hands, therefore, the shift of focus from the *orchestra* to the *skene* becomes fully apparent. The *skene* itself looms larger in Euripides' mind. For Aeschylus it was a conventional background that could be imagined away at will. For Euripides it is a permanent and very solid structure whose visible presence cannot be denied, and which must be accounted for in the drama. In Aeschylus the play dictates the setting, but in Euripides the setting begins to dictate the play. What had originally been a conventional arrangement of acting levels is now visualized as the realistic representation of a house: what had once been "heaven" is now a roof on which characters may climb, and the *skene* doors are often specified as leading into actual rooms inside. Undoubtedly Euripides is influenced by the greater literalness of comedy. We have already noted the scenic arrangements for Aristophanes' *The Clouds,* where the *skene* roof represents that of Socrates' Academy. *Lysistrata* is another case in point: here the upper story stands for the Acropolis, the central doors for the Propylaea, and the steps leading to the stage for the hill up which the old men have to climb. Euripides' use of the levels in his *Orestes* reveals the same mode of thought. The basic structure is the same, but the tragic playwright's attitude to it has radically changed.

Thus we find, far more frequently in Euripides than in other writers, that the *skene* is identified from the outset as a specific building, and that the action rarely shifts from the limits originally established. Though Euripides, when his plot demands it, can still avail himself of the old, convenient ambiguity (as in the vagueness of *Hecuba,* see p. 32), it is with him that the so-called "unity of place" finds its greatest justification. His characters are more earthbound in their interests and motivations, and his setting, brought into greater prominence and urging stricter limitations upon them, reflects this narrowing of focus.

We may consider two specific examples of this greater scenic literalness. The first is from *Helen,* Euripides' unorthodox retelling of the genesis of the Trojan War. In this version, Helen did not go with Paris to Troy. Only her god-created simulacrum was taken, while the real lady was spirited away to Egypt. The action is laid before the Pharaoh's palace. On his first entrance, Theoclymenos delivers a eulogy over his father's tomb:

> All hail, my father's monument. It was for this
> I had you buried, Proteus, at my door:
> That at my coming in and going forth
> I might address you. Father, it is I,
> Yes, Theoclymenos, your son, who speaks.
>
> [vv. 1165 ff.]

The explanation is surely dictated by the conventional features of the setting. What these features were we have already seen in *The Libation Bearers:* a permanent stage altar which could represent a tomb, and the *skene* door, which stood for the palace gates. In Aeschylus' hands they provided what Nagler has called "polyscenic juxtaposition," like the simultaneous staging of the Middle Ages, in which either element could be called into use as the action demanded, with the other allowed to lapse into oblivion. Euripides views the arrangement more literally and is uncomfortable with it, for in real life one does not normally bury one's father on one's doorstep. He therefore feels impelled to write these few lines of justification, which, as usual, only make the convention more obvious by trying to explain it away. Nineteenth-century producers of Shakespeare fell into similar traps when trying to give concrete form to the poet's scenic imaginings. Theatrical historians have reason to be grateful to Euripides; often, in his attempts to disguise the features of his stage, he only succeeds in bringing them more forcibly to our attention.

The second example occurs in our only complete surviving satyr play, Euripides' *Cyclops.* Here the *skene* represents the cave of Polyphemus on the coast of Sicily and is so identified by Silenus early in the Prologue. Odysseus and his sailors are driven inside by their cannibalistic captor. After a lugubrious song by the satyr chorus, Odysseus reappears to report the horrible events inside. He concludes thus:

> I'll not seek safety by deserting my friends,
> Though escape I could, for I crept outside
> Through a rift in the rock, and the rest are within.
> Shall I alone live, and relinquish the friends
> In whose company I came? It would be a crime.
>
> [vv. 478 ff.]

As before, this literalness is largely self-defeating. We wonder why, if Odysseus could slip out through a convenient crevice, his companions could not do the same. Aeschylus would not have felt compelled to justify Odysseus' reappearance in this way, any more than he feels the need to explain, in *Agamemnon*, how the Herald can apparently journey from Troy to Argos almost as fast as the chain of beacon-fires. It is typical of Euripides' preconceptions that he feels such explanations to be necessary.

Together with the literalness of place, we see in the later plays of Euripides an increasing literalness of time. When Aeschylus wishes to show us that it is night, he tells us so. Thus the Prologue of *Agamemnon*:

> Gods, hear my prayer; release me from this drudgery,
> This long twelvemonth I have watched here, couched
> On the roof of Atreus' palace like a dog,
> And marked the nightly concourse of the stars
> Around their bright lords blazoned in the sky
> That usher in our summers and our snows.
> And now I await the message written in flame,
> The gleam of fire that brings report from Troy
> That she is taken . . .
>
> I give you welcome, beacon! You have brought
> Light to our darkness, and Argos in your honor
> Will ring with choruses and dancing feet.

It is all in the words, and no visual indication is necessary. In Euripides' *Iphigeneia in Aulis*, however, night is established in the

Elizabethan manner, by a lamp standing on the stage. In *Rhesus* the whole chorus carries lighted torches. We may note that in earlier tragedy the torch normally had a symbolic value. It was the traditional apparatus of the Furies. Thus *The Eumenides;* thus also Cassandra, who exercises a Fury-like function in *The Trojan Women.* The more literal use of torch or lamp to indicate darkness is originally comic. Strepsiades, at the beginning of *The Clouds,* lies tossing and turning in his bed and finally, unable to sleep, orders his slave to bring the lamp. In a lost play by Aristophanes entitled *Dramata* or *Niobos,* a lamp has just been extinguished in a scuffle. The conspiring women in *Ekklesiazousai* (*The Congresswomen*) carry lanterns to show that it is not yet daybreak. The practice becomes commonplace in fourth-century comedy. Its use in tragedy shows the gradual shift toward a greater degree of illusion. The view held by some critics that the two examples quoted from Euripides were not originally penned by that poet but by a later imitator of his style do not materially affect the argument. Whoever wrote these scenes thought such a device necessary to inform the audience of the supposed time of the action.

The same philosophy influences Euripides' approach to stage costuming. Our scanty information suggests that this had already undergone some modification since Aeschylus' time: Sophocles, for example, is credited with introducing a new type of footwear. But Euripides' innovations were of a different quality. It seems clear that he introduced a greater note of realism, which at first seemed revolutionary but was subsequently imitated by his contemporaries. Our evidence here comes almost entirely from Aristophanes, who devotes one scene to the subject in his earliest extant comedy, *The Acharnians.* (See discussion of this scene in Chapter Two.) Dikaiopolis, the pacifist hero, needs to work on the sympathies of a bellicose chorus, and goes to Euripides to borrow a suit of tragic rags. The petulant playwright suggests various suitable characters from his plays—Oineus, Phoenix, Philoctetes, Bellerophon, Thyestes, Ino, and Telephus. It seems clear from the text that all the costumes are on view. Dikaiopolis happily chooses the last as the most pathetic. He then demands suitable properties, growing so importunate that Euripides retires in pique. Dressed in his borrowed shabbiness, Dikaiopolis can return to the chorus with greater confidence.

The tone of the scene suggests that Aristophanes is dealing with an aspect of Euripidean tragedy well known to the audience, and that the tragedian, early in his career (*Telephus* was produced in 438, as part of the revolutionary bill that included *Alcestis* instead of the usual satyr play) had modified the old formality of costume into a greater realism. Exactly how far these modifications went we cannot say. Iris Brooke has argued that the differences between Euripides' costumes and those of his predecessors were "as marked as the differences between the designs used by Charles Kean and those of Gordon Craig"; but this is probably an overstatement. In a theatre as tradition-bound as the Greek, any change provoked comment, and Euripides' costumes would probably not strike us as unduly realistic by modern standards. Nor was Euripides the innovator in this. Aeschylus had shown a ragged Xerxes in *The Persians,* written in 472. But in this case the value of the costume was largely symbolic. Xerxes in his torn robes stands for the destruction of the Persian army; and it has been suggested that, at the end of the play, he changed into the new finery that Atossa the queen-mother had earlier promised to bring him, as a reminder to the Athenian audience that decimated battalions could be replenished and the Persian menace was not yet dead. (Another possibility is that Xerxes entered in traditional stage finery, carrying the ragged costume with him.) Euripides uses rags more freely and with a greater eye to their emotive effect. This was seen by the critics as yet another example of the degradation of tragedy: Aristophanes, in a complex allusion, refers to Euripides as "the beggar-poet." As the years passed, however, the device became more familiar. Sophocles showed a ragged Philoctetes in 414. Euripides seems to have dressed his Philoctetes in beast skins, though the date of his play is indeterminate. We may say at least that what was condemned as unorthodox in 438 was respectable twenty years later. It is significant that, although Aristophanes returns to the issue in *The Frogs* (405), it is here a minor matter, one small charge among many, and not worth dwelling on for too long. The shock value had diminished.

Other aspects of this change appear. As part of his realistic design, Euripides set great store by local color. We see this in *Medea*, where the foreignness of the protagonist is stressed throughout and was apparently reinforced, at the original production, by an exotic costume. Our evidence comes from vase painting, which, as we have seen, often took its inspiration from theatrical sources. Before 431, the year in which the play appeared, illustrations of the Medea theme show the Colchian princess in conventional Greek dress. Those appearing afterward favor an oriental costume. It seems more than likely that this change was inspired by Euripides' innovations. Medea was a barbarian; and barbarians, in general, fascinated him. The Thracian Polymestor and his escort in *Hecuba*, the savage Thoas in *Iphigeneia in Tauris*, and the Egyptians of *Helen* are examples. From Aristophanic strictures we may gather that he dressed them appropriately. The bizarrely costumed Persians and Thracians in *The Acharnians* are jokes at Euripides' expense, and the references to "Euripidean savages" in *Lysistrata* clearly struck a responsive chord in the Athenian audience.

Not the least important of Euripides' characteristics, and a further way in which his influence made itself felt, was his addiction to spectacle. We have seen how he was responsible for developing, if not originating, the use of the *mechane* for quasi-realistic effects. In Aeschylus, a certain spectacular effect had been provided by the large choruses, but Euripides, whose choruses are smaller and less important, more than compensates for this in other ways. Euripides loved crowd scenes, and was more extravagant in his use of extras than any other dramatist we know. His plays are full of processions. In *Electra*, Clytemnestra enters in a chariot with her retinue; the same happens in *Iphigeneia in Aulis*. *The Trojan Women* and *Rhesus* have elaborate processional entrances. In *Helen*, the priestess Theonoe is accompanied by a train of handmaidens bearing lighted torches, and Theoclymenos by huntsmen with the appropriate equipment. There are funeral processions in *Alcestis, Andromache, Bacchae, Electra, Hecuba, The Phoenician Women,* and *The Suppliant Women.* The entrance of the Corpse in Aristophanes' *The Frogs* burlesques the typical tragic cortege. In Euripides' hands the stage was already acquiring that love of spectacle for its own sake that was to be the hallmark of Hellenistic tragedy.

The Actor

With the shift of focus from *orchestra* to *skene* and the gradual withdrawal of the playwright into the purely literary domain, the actor acquired increasing importance. Aristotle was to lament that the theatre, which in the fifth century had belonged to the poets, was dominated by actors in the fourth; and even in the fifth century we can trace an increasing interest in the actors' individual personalities. They were no longer, as with Aeschylus, mere mouthpieces for the playwright. They became artists in their own right, interpreters with their own distinctive contributions to make.

This was partially due to the new demands made on the actor by the playwright. He had more to do. Though the general characteristics of Greek acting examined in Chapter Two still obtained through Euripides' time, some changes are evident. Our sources suggest that fifth-century acting, at first comparatively statuesque, demanded considerably more in the way of movement as the years went on. Mynniskos, who had acted for Aeschylus and whose name first appears in the records about 445, was severely critical of Callippides, who belonged to the next generation and acted for Euripides among others. Aristotle quotes Mynniskos twice, first as accusing Callippides of using excessive action, and later as saying that the younger actor, like his contemporaries, did not play female roles as if they were gentlewomen. In Greek terms, these two criticisms amounted to the same thing: a well-brought-up lady was expected to move with decorum and make herself as inconspicuous as possible. The charge underlying this criticism is borne out by the plays. Aeschylus' tragedies are virtually static, while those of Euripides demand much more in the way of violent stage action. That Aristotle shared Mynniskos' disapproval of the increasing mobility of the actor is plain to see. In the *Poetics* he illustrates the difference between epic and tragedy by comparing them to the old and new schools of acting respectively; the old, he says, made its effect without the lavish use of gesture which characterized the new. He recognizes a certain amount of gesture as essential—he advises the poet, in fact, as an aid to composition, to act out the story with the very gestures of his actors, but insists that tragedy may produce its effect with the minimum of movement or action, like epic, and that the fault lies with the interpreters, not with the poet. In view of the parallel already noted between acting and rhetoric, it is interesting to see that the fourth century applied a similar criticism to the gestures of oratory. We possess the comment of Aeschines, Demosthenes' opponent and Aristotle's contemporary: "The orators of past generations, Pericles, Themistocles, Aristides, had too much restraint to do what we all do now as a matter of habit, namely, to speak with the hand outside the robe. They thought this unseemly, and took care to avoid it." In other words, the fourth-century orator used a profusion of gesture where his predecessors had used little or none. Aristotle even extends the same criticism to singing and the recitation of epic in his time. The performer was beginning to assert himself.

Sophocles is said to have been the first to compose parts with particular actors in mind. We may perhaps see the effect of this in, for instance, the similarity between Creon in *Antigone* and Menelaus in *Ajax*, plays written at about the same time. At any rate, the bare statement is evidence that, even so early, the personality of the actor was beginning to affect the work of the dramatist. This question is particularly intriguing in Euripides, notably in those "split action" plays, where the tragedy is clearly divided into two parts with identical structure but different characters, and one half is intended to be balanced against the other. If we analyze the part division of *Hecuba*, it seems likely that Hecuba's two archenemies, Odysseus in the first half of the play and Polymestor in the second, were played by the same actor. The point of the tragedy would be even stronger if the actor's personality was strong enough to make this apparent. *The Madness of Heracles* has the same basic structure. In the first half, Heracles' family is threatened with shameful death by the tyrant Lycus. The hero arrives in the nick of time to save them. In the second half, Heracles, now insane, brings upon his wife and children the same death he had thwarted earlier. Euripides' point is that even the noblest and most self-sufficient of men is liable to the arbitrary reversals of fortune. The part division has an obvious thematic function, for Lycus and Heracles must be played by the same actor (Lycus has already left when Heracles arrives, and they meet offstage only); as in *Hecuba*, its value would be even greater if the personality of the actor were allowed to shine through the mask.

It is significant that we know more personal details about the later fifth-century actors than about their predecessors. This is not entirely a matter of more vivid record keeping. Aeschylus' Mynniskos is a shadowy figure compared with his successors; the growing interest in personalities is symptomatic of the trend. We hear of Molon, who acted for Euripides and was famous for his size; he played Phoenix in the tragedy of that name. We hear of Pleisthenes, who acted in the *Ajax* of Carcinus and whose striking laugh inspired another proverb.

Thus, with the fourth century, we see the emergence of a star system and a theatre dominated by virtuosi who subordinated the play to their own talents. It is a familiar process. The same thing happened to Shakespeare in the centuries after his death, and audiences who had once gone to see *Macbeth* now flocked to hear David Garrick. In the Greek theatre, this new kind of actor was exemplified by the famous Theodorus. According to Aristotle, he insisted on always being the first actor to appear in the play, on the theory that audiences were more responsive to first impressions. It is not quite clear how he accomplished this. We know, for example, that he played Hecuba in Euripides' tragedy of that name; but the play begins with a Prologue spoken by the ghost of Polydorus, whose exit is followed immediately by Hecuba's entrance. Either Theodorus demonstrated his versatility by a rapid change, or, more likely, adapted the play to suit his vanity. By this period the scripts of the old masters were subject to the actor's whim; again, the parallel with the history of Shakespearean production is evident. It was the age of revivals, and the stars had no compunction in rewriting to suit their talents and resources. Ad-libbing must always have been practiced to a certain extent, particularly in comedy, where actors were not slow to interrupt the action with their favorite pieces of business—for example, the story of Hermon and his stick, already quoted. For tragedy, we possess an amusing parody of the actor's habit of interlarding his speeches with extraneous moans and groans. But by the fourth century this tendency had run wild. Things reached such a state that the Athenian authorities were compelled to launch a preservation movement, prepare official texts of the old plays, and deposit copies in the city archives, admonishing actors that they must adhere to them in the future. It is from these official copies, spirited away to the library of Alexandria, that our own texts ultimately derive. Even here, however, it is possible to detect many places where actors' interpolations have become embedded in the original script.

To this period also belong the displays of vocal virtuosity that Plato criticizes so severely. The fourth-century actor, like the fourth-century sculptor and painter, was increasingly preoccupied with technique. On one level, this produced a far greater degree of realistic impersonation. It was remarked of Theodorus that his voice always seemed to belong to his characters, while those of his fellows seemed to be assumed. But it also produced cadenzas, flourishes, and extraneous impersonations of an alarming kind. This was the type of vulgar display to which Plato objected:

And other types of men will be all the more ready to vary their style the worse they are, and will think nothing beneath them. They will seriously try to represent in public all the things we were talking about. We shall have the noises of thunder and wind and hail, and of axles and wheels, the notes of trumpets, pipes, whistles, and every possible instrument, the barking of dogs, the bleating of sheep and twittering of birds. All these will be represented by voice and gesture, and narrative will play but a small part.

Plato's strictures, though exaggerated to make a point, had their basis in fact. A Theodorus—probably the famous one—was known for his imitation of the windlass. Parmenon was equally famous for imitating pigs. Hence comes the story that Parmenon's rivals brought a real pig into the auditorium; when it squealed the audience shouted "Good, but nothing like Parmenon." The pig was then released and Parmenon's supporters confounded.

Changes in a Commercial Theatre

By the fourth century, the theatre had become commercial. Inaugurated as part of a sacred rite, it had grown increasingly more secular as the fifth century progressed. Some critics have hailed this tension as the source of the theatre's creative vitality. But by the fourth century the secular predominated. Although the major dramatic festivals continued in existence, and were to do so through Roman times, touring companies were now taking plays through Greece and the colonies, performing wherever and whenever an audience could be found. There was some precedent for this. Even in the fifth century, actors and playwrights had been in demand for visiting engagements. Nikostratos the Athenian had been hired to act in Aetolia. Aeschylus had taken some of his productions to Sicily, where they were performed in the great Theatre of Syracuse. It was during such a visit that he died. Euripides, from choice or necessity, had gone to work in Macedonia. But by the fourth century, touring had become an important economic factor in theatrical life. We may take the career of Aeschines, who later earned reflected glory as Demosthenes' chief political opponent, as typical. Born in 390, he must have been a young actor of considerable promise, for he attracted the attention of Theodorus and Aristodemus, two of the greatest actors of the time, and was taken into their companies for important roles in classic revivals.

Demosthenes sneers at him as a third-rate actor, telling a malicious story of how he tripped in one performance and was prevented by his heavy costume from struggling to his feet. But he had some good parts: the title roles in Euripides' *Oinomaos* and *Kresphontes,* now lost; Thyestes in *Kressai;* Polydorus in *Hecuba;* and possibly Creon in *Antigone* and Talthybius or Menelaus in *The Trojan Women.* His theatrical fortunes, however, fluctuated. At some point in his career he joined an inferior company and played his parts "while collecting figs, grapes, and olives, like a produce merchant, from other people's gardens, and getting more from this source than from your dramatic contests." Did the company subsist mainly on charity, and was Aeschines deputed to go out and beg for food? Or is Demosthenes implying that he lived off the fruit with which the audience pelted him? Much of this is undoubtedly rhetorical exaggeration, and Demosthenes repeatedly pays tribute to a quality which must have assisted Aeschines in politics as well as on the stage, his fine voice. Nevertheless Demosthenes' abuse has its own interest. It shows the new status which the actor was forced to accept along with his professionalism. Aeschines is "an ape" (we must remember how frequently this derogatory term has been used of actors, for instance in Molière's time) and his mother is "a lunch-hour prostitute."

It is apparent that the theatrical profession had now begun to carry a certain stigma, which was to endure throughout Roman times. By turning professional the actor had forfeited public esteem. "Why" asks Aristotle "are Dionysiac artists usually disreputable characters? Is it because they have least share in the theory of wisdom, since most of their life is spent in arts which they practice for a living, and because much of their life is spent in incontinence, and some in dire straits? Both these conditions are productive of inferiority." Elsewhere he asks why men should accept the degradation of working as conjurers, actors or pipers when they could pursue such honorable professions as astronomy or oratory. The actors sought professional security in guilds organized on geographical lines, which, somewhat in the manner of Actors' Equity, laid down rules for conduct and employment.

Claiming religious immunity as the sacred servants of Dionysos, they enjoyed international protection. There is a continuous record of grants of immunity by individual city-states; such privileges were liable to be forfeited if the artists failed to observe the terms of their contracts. The well-known "House of Masks" excavated on the island of Delos was probably a guild center in connection with the local festival, which also offered facilities for rehearsals. A mosaic floor shows Dionysos in tragic costume riding on a leopard, with pictures of masks and musicians. Under the protection of the guilds, leading players could still enjoy considerable prestige and earn the inflated salaries that we now associate with opera stars. They could still occasionally be entrusted with important diplomatic missions where their rhetorical ability would be useful. Ischandros was brought by Aeschines before the Athenian assembly to present political proposals from a sympathetic faction in Arcadia. Aristodemos was sent on missions to Philip, and Neoptolemos was influential in persuading the Athenians to accept Philip's peace. Thettalos went as Alexander's emissary to Caria, and in the latter part of the third century, Ariston of Syracuse served as a spokesman before his city's authorities. But the average player was learning to suffer the odium, explicit or unspoken, that is still his lot today.

Choice of Plays

The new organizational pattern of the theatre influenced the choice of plays, which in turn influenced the development of stage architecture. Original tragedies of the fourth century and later borrowed heavily from the more superficial aspects of Euripidean technique: violence, showmanship, love of spectacle for its own sake. Revivals of older plays (the first attested example at the Athens festival was in 386) adopted the same characteristics. Aeschylus was out of fashion. It was no longer easy to mount plays which relied so extensively on a powerful chorus: we know that some companies at least had by now reduced the number of the chorus to nine. Many plays of Sophocles were still in the repertoire, but Euripides, suspect in the fifth century, was the chief favorite of the fourth and long afterward, not least because he wrote good showy parts for actors. Such revivals, at least in the main festival centers, were geared to the new vogue for spectacle. Later productions of *Agamemnon* seem to have increased the number of chariots used for the King's entrance. In *The Eumenides*, Athena entered "flying" on the *mechane*, instead of on the *skene* roof or in a chariot as before. A revival of Euripides' *Orestes* opened, in defiance of the text, with an extraneous procession of the spoils of Troy. We may trace the changing fashion in revivals of Sophocles' *Ajax*. In the original production the hero's suicide took place offstage: he was probably whisked out of sight by the *ekkyklema* (wagon-stage) at the crucial moment. Later audiences were offered a more realistic spectacle, achieved by a telescoping sword and, probably, bladders of stage blood. The prima donna temperaments of actors contributed to this spectacular extravagance. We are told of one player who refused to go on in a royal part unless he was given a sufficient retinue.

Tragedy, however, claimed an increasingly smaller share of the public attention. The favored form now was comedy, a type of comedy far different from that which Aristophanes had written, which reflected a Greece whose aims and aspirations had changed, and a theatre which had resigned itself to the mere provision of entertainment. Fifth-century Greece had been a conglomeration of independent city-states, each fiercely concerned with local politics and personalities and parochial in its humor. Aristophanes had written for an Athenian audience preoccupied with its own problems and receptive to satire of its leaders and institutions. With the conquests of Alexander, which gave Greece a greater cohesion than it had ever enjoyed before and imposed Greek culture on traditional enemies, the pattern changed. The players, already accustomed to touring in Greece itself, now followed in the wake of the armies. Persia now became familiar territory, as southern Italy had been before; the influence of the Greek theatre reached as far as India, where it made its mark on native drama forms. Plays whose appeal was limited to one small community were no longer viable; an audience in Ephesus or Alexandria could not be expected to laugh at the antics of a comic Socrates. Comedy turned to subject matter that was universally appreciable, with plots that turned on familiar domestic situations and settings that sought to reproduce the everyday background of the city street.

Stage Architecture

For this purpose, the existing form of the *skene*, which had by now, if not before, acquired three doors, was already suitable. We have seen how Euripides transformed the *skene*, without modifying its structure, into an approximation to a realistic setting. With the advent of New Comedy—by which we mean the work of Menander, Diphilos, Philemon, and their contemporaries—the transformation from a presentational to a representational theatre is virtually complete. The stage now almost invariably represents a street, and the *skene* doors the houses fronting on it. Identified early in the comedy, they retain the same identity throughout. Our direct evidence for New Comedy is scanty; we possess only three complete plays and substantial fragments of others by Menander, and virtually nothing by his contemporaries. Most of our knowledge is derived from the later Roman imitations. Menander's plays, however, tell us all we need to know. In the recently discovered *Dyskolos* (*The Grouch*), the god Pan, who speaks the Prologue, identifies the three doors in the opening lines:

> Imagine now we are in Attica,
> At Phyle; and this cave from which I enter
> Is sacred to the nymphs. The people here—
> All who can scratch a living from these rocks—
> Hold it in particular esteem.
> The farmhouse on my right belongs to Knemon,
> A man who hates the human race, who shuns
> All company, and won't give anyone
> So much as a good-day.

Pan goes on to relate how Knemon's wife, finding her marriage intolerable,

> *left him, and went back*
> *To her son by a former marriage. This little place*
> *Next door belongs to him; and there he makes*
> *A bare subsistence for himself, his mother*
> *And a single faithful slave, who used to be*
> *His father's.*

The arrangement is clear. Pan's grotto is represented by the center door: although he never reappears after the Prologue, his spirit continues to preside over the play. The flanking doors represent the farms of Knemon and Gorgias, respectively. In Chapter One, mention was made of the theory that the earliest informing image for the *skene* was the conventional structure of an actual shrine, with a central niche or archway holding the effigy of the god. The arrangement for *Dyskolos,* paralleled in other New Comic plays, may preserve a memory of this, particularly since the permanent stage altar still seems to have been present before the central doors. An ancient summary of Menander's *The Ghost* shows that the action requires two houses separated by a central shrine "hung with branches"; the fragmentary Prologue specifically mentions the altar. Other plays of Menander require only ordinary house fronts. *Perikeiromene (The Rape of the Locks)* needs three—for the soldier Polemon, the merchant Pataikos, and Myrrhine, a lady of Corinth, where the play is set. Where only two houses were required—as, for instance, in *The Arbitration*—one door could simply be closed off for the action of the play.

The Chorus

Besides a change of scenic attitude, the later Greek theatre also shows a change of form. The stage was increased in height to give greater prominence to the actors. Vitruvius' later description specifies this height as "not less than ten, and not more than twelve

feet." Although steps continued to link stage and *orchestra*, this
new elevation imposed greater restraint on actor-chorus interac-
tion. The chorus, however, now had little to do with the drama, at
least in its more popular form. In the early fourth century, Aristophanes in comedy and Agathon in tragedy had already given up
writing special material for the choruses to sing. They substituted
ready-made lyrics (*embolima*) drawn from stock, with no particular relevance to the play. In some cases the presence of the chorus
is betrayed only by a marginal annotation in the text. In *Dyskolos*,
the function of the chorus is solely to provide musical entr'actes,
during which the stage is empty of characters. From this it was
but a short step to the elimination of the chorus altogether. It
continued to survive in tragedy, as we know from mentions in
official decrees. In Hellenistic times there is still evidence for cho-
rus-masters (*chorodidaskaloi*); inscriptions found at Tanagra and
dating from the first century B.C. attest to the presence of choruses
there, and, though the practice differed from one community to
another, choruses were still known in Rome well into imperial
times. In comedy, however, the chorus was only occasionally present, if at all; and the *orchestra*, which in the fifth century had
been the center of attention, was now largely a void, a mystic gulf
separating the spectators from the performance.

We may see in these changes the logical development of the
innovations introduced by Euripides. It is perhaps no accident
that this man, if the traditions are to be believed, seems to have
been the first Greek dramatist to have conceived of the playwright
as a being apart, a "professional" almost in the modern sense, and
deliberately to have restricted his involvement in public affairs so
that he could concentrate on writing. The plays, like their author,
deliberately removed themselves from the public they sought to
impress and instruct. Although Euripides attempted to bring the
drama closer to contemporary sensibilities by using new language,
new adaptations of the stories, and new lines of attack, his unex-
ampled naturalism served, paradoxically, to make the plays more
remote. His dramas seek constantly to persuade the audience that
they are elsewhere than where they are, not watching a play in a

theatre but observing real people in real locations, participating in actions that belong not to myth but to real life. We observe too, as the years go by, the growing specialization of the performer into a man who devotes his life to acting and has his own private lore and training which set him apart from the nonprofessional.

In the fourth century, the chorus, that important point of contact between the public and the play, almost entirely vanishes. The *orchestra* becomes a void, infringed upon on one side by the spreading *skene* and on the other by additional seating. This change is reflected in the confusion of theatrical terminology. With the late Greek and Latin writers, *orchestra*, which in the earliest theatre had been synonymous with the principal acting area, now comes to mean "stage." The Hellenistic theatre looks toward the modern proscenium-stage pattern in which the spectators are separated from the action by both spatial and psychological barriers, and observe the play as a remote spectacle, no longer as something within the compass of their own group. In its developing physical form, the Greek theatre provides an architectural metaphor of the growing estrangement of drama from society. Menander's stage is the logical descendant of Euripides', just as his comedies, on his own admission, were inspired by the techniques of Euripidean tragedy.

Hellenistic Theatre Building

Surviving examples of Hellenistic theatre building are comparatively plentiful and show clearly the changes that were taking place. When the Athenian statesman Lycurgus, who had also been responsible for preparing the authorized versions of the classical plays, had the Theatre of Dionysos remodeled between 338 and 326, he did little more than rebuild in stone, and with a more grandiose appearance, the basic structure as Sophocles had known it. At about the same time the architect Polycleitos (not to be confused with the famous sculptor of the same name) designed the great Theatre of Epidauros, in the Argolid. This deserves special discussion, not only as the best preserved example of Greek theatre building still to survive in our time, and in regular use for revivals of classical drama, but as a structure which keeps faith with the old age while looking forward to the new.

Epidauros was the Greek Lourdes, a healing shrine dedicated to the god Asklepios, whose international importance more than justified the building of an impressive theatre. This was located some distance from the principal shrine complex in a perfect natural setting, the northeast slope of Mount Kynortion, which was steep enough to support a large auditorium, and at the same time low enough to remain unobtrusive. Here Polycleitos laid out his *orchestra* in a perfect circle: it is the only such form which survives in Greece. Its center is marked by a round stone with a small circular table or socket. This is usually interpreted as the base of the orchestral altar; it may, however, have been simply an architect's device for drawing the audience's attention to the focal point and to provide a marker for the choral dances. The *orches-*

Athens, Theatre of Dionysos.
View from the Acropolis, showing
Hellenistic and Roman modifications.

tra is rimmed by a gutter of flat stones, which both carries off rainwater and gives access to the seats of honor in the lowest tier. The auditorium, slightly larger than a semicircle, is divided into upper and lower sections by a lateral gangway; each section is further divided into wedges by ascending aisles, with twenty-two wedges in the upper section and twelve in the lower. In ancient times, the total seating capacity was somewhere between twelve and fourteen thousand. Even more have been squeezed in for modern gala performances.

The *skene* consisted basically of one large room, flanked by antechambers, which were presumably used for costumes and storage. (The large towers built outside the auditorium limits may have had the same purpose, and perhaps doubled as guard houses.) In front of this was a raised stage 10 feet 4 inches deep and 11 feet 6 inches high. These dimensions, however, derive from what appears to be a second-century reconstruction: the original stage may have been rather lower. It was approached on either side by earth ramps between stone walls. At the end of each ramp, at ground level, was a double arch, one half giving access to the ramp itself, the other leading into the *orchestra* to provide a *parodos*. One of these archways was restored when the theatre was put back into service. Small sockets in the stonework suggest that the openings were closed off by curtains during the performance so that the audience would not see the chorus assembling outside.

The Theatre of Epidauros as used for the modern festivals provides a vivid evocation of what the ancient performances must have been. Plays, which are now given in the evenings, use the full resources of modern stage lighting; this at least means that the drama no longer has to compete with the beauty of the natural setting for attention. The *skene* facade is rebuilt and changes to suit the particular play—a technique the Greeks had probably already begun to use when Epidauros was first constructed. And the action is sometimes allowed to spread out onto the enclosing hill, so that gods and goddesses, instead of appearing aloft on the *skene*, are seen isolated in pools of light among the trees. The present productions at Epidauros, the work of the Greek National Theatre, represent an effective compromise between old and new ideas.

Other important theatres date from the same period. At Delphi, one of the best preserved, the *orchestra* and auditorium date from the late fourth century. Here the builders were, in one sense, less fortunate; the awesome mountains overwhelm the site, while the theatre seems cramped for space and the seating precipitous. The stage buildings were reconstructed between 160 and 158 B.C.: the *skene* shows the same arrangement as at Epidauros, with one large room and flanking smaller rooms. Like Epidauros too, Delphi still houses modern revivals. In a recent production of *Prometheus Bound,* eagles from the surrounding mountains added an eery dimension to the play when they swooped and circled over the *orchestra.*

On the Turkish coast a few miles from the island of Samos,

Theatre of Epidauros,
restored for the annual Festival of Ancient Drama.
[Courtesy of the Greek National Tourist Office]

excavators have uncovered the greater part of the Greek city of Priene. Its theatre, of which extensive remains have survived, is of particular interest, allowing as it does a more complete reconstruction of the Hellenistic *skene*, and showing the new developments in the *orchestra*. Under construction perhaps as early as 340, the theatre was intimate by Greek standards, holding a mere 5,000 people. For some time it doubled as the meeting place of the city, thus preserving a connection which had once been vital to the Greek theatre but had now almost entirely disappeared. Many of the details are unclear, but the general pattern is obvious. The *skene* and its associated stage now thrust boldly out into the *orchestra* circle. It seems almost certain that doors in the lower level of the *skene* offered direct access to the *orchestra*, so that this area was still available for playing. In this case the raised stage would have been high enough for its facade to provide a background for the action, as the old *skene* had done before. The raised stage itself, however, was the favorite site for comic performances.

On the other side of the *orchestra*, seats have begun to creep into the circle. These were thrones of honor, set apart from the mass of the spectators. A similar arrangement was used in the later reconstruction of the Theatre of Oropos, in Attica. These seats had one obvious disadvantage. When the high stage was used, they gave a poor view of the performance. Although dignitaries go to the theatre as much to be seen as to see (royal boxes in European theatres usually have the worst view in the house), the city fathers of Priene were obviously sensitive about this. At a later date, new seats of honor were erected half-way back in the auditorium at the foot of the upper section, so that their proud occupiers now had an excellent view of the show.

The Theatre of Delos, the island sacred to the god Apollo and the site of international festivals, is interesting not only in its own right but for the records preserved with it, which give details of construction and repairs. There may have been a wooden *skene* here from the fourth century. Perhaps about 274, it was converted into stone, the cost being borne by the treasury of Apollo. Once again the theatre was a small one, with a capacity little greater than Priene's. We know from the surviving records, however, that it possessed elaborate scenic resources. For the first time *skene* begins to mean "scenery" in our modern sense of the word. The earliest recorded example at Delos is from 296 B.C. In the plural form, *skenai*, the word came to mean painted panels which could be changed from play to play. Decorating these panels was expensive, as the records show; in the second century, a special scene shop (*skenotheke*) was erected for the purpose.

The accounts for 274 give instructions for repairing the *exostra*, stairway and altars. What the *exostra* was is not quite clear. Literary references suggest that it may have been a stage machine similar in function to the *ekkyklema*. The stairway mentioned was presumably either that connecting the stage with the *orchestra* level, or another giving access to the different stories of the *skene* itself. The reference to "altars" in the plural is suggestive. It implies that the stage, or property, altar was still present, as well as the second altar that marked the center of the *orchestra* circle.

We have noted the changing sense of the word *skene* to conform to the new theatre practice. The Delian inscriptions also provide us with a new technical term which has become embedded in our theatre: *proskenion*, which first appears about 300 B.C., and again in 282. Here the contractor is commissioned to provide "screens for the proscenium" (*pinakas eis to proskenion*). *Pinakes* here is obviously equivalent to *skenai*, and means the changeable painted panels which could be inserted between permanent uprights to change the scene. *Proskenion*, which means literally "something set up before the *skene*," normally denotes the scenic facade. Antiphanes, a comic poet of the fourth centurys, applied the term metaphorically to the prostitute Nannion, whose beauty, it seems, was not even skin deep. Apparently the decoration of the *proskenion* was not necessarily related to the play. Athenaeus, a prolific writer of the second century A.D., who has left us fifteen books of academic gossip, mentions that a picture of Demetrius Poliorketes ("The Besieger") adorned the *proskenion* of the Theatre of Dionysos in Athens; and Demetrius and Menander were contemporaries. Both Plautus and Vitruvius, however, clearly use the Latin form, *proscaenium,* to mean "stage" (which is also, though in a different sense, "something set up before the *skene*"); and the modern derivation has come to acquire yet another meaning, the picture-frame arch which encloses the stage.

Hellenistic Stage Machinery

The Hellenistic theatre was mechanically minded. Our literary sources describe, in more or less detail, various types of stage machinery, though without assigning them to any particular period. Both Pollux and Vitruvius describe devices for changing scenery, known as *periaktoi.* In Pollux we read:

By each of the two doors on either side of the center door there would be two others, one on each side, against which the *periaktoi* were fixed. That on the right shows things outside, that on the left things from the city, particularly from the seashore. It brings in sea-gods and whatever is too heavy for the *mechane* to carry. If the *periaktoi* revolve, that on the right changes the district, while both change the country.

Vitruvius' description is a little more precise:

The Greeks call these places *periaktoi* because there are revolving contrivances there, each having three sides and different sorts of decoration on each. When the story is about to change, or a god is about to arrive, they revolve with a sudden noise of thunder and change the decoration on the front.

Exactly what these writers mean is difficult to determine. Pollux is particularly confusing. In general terms, they seem to be referring to revolving, prism-shaped structures with a different design on each face (Pollux tells us elsewhere that the panels were removable) that could turn to show, or at least suggest, changes of locality. It seems from Pollux that they could also serve as revolving stages to bring on characters, somewhat in the manner of the small revolves in the traditional Japanese Kabuki theatre. Pollux also appears to be suggesting a convention whereby, if one *periaktos* turned, only a slight change of scene was indicated, while the operation of both indicated a complete shift. It has indeed been suggested that these devices were already in use in the fifth century and were used, for example, in *Ajax*, to indicate the shift from Ajax's tent to the seashore. This is merely unsupported surmise, however, and everything we know about the fifth-century theatre argues against the use of such elaborate mechanics so early. Archaeologists have uncovered what may be the supports for such structures in later theatres. At Oropos, stones set at either end of the later *proskenion* foundations carry sockets or pivot-holes. Similar stones have been found in the Greek-inspired theatre at Pompeii. The position of the *periaktoi* probably varied from one theatre to another. Pollux and Vitruvius both seem to indicate that they were housed in recesses on the *skene* wall. The Renaissance scholar-designers who tried to recreate the form of the classical theatre and restored the *periaktoi* to practical use themselves found the ancient directions confusing. An illustrated Italian edition of Vitruvius shows a *periaktos* behind each of the three principal doors. It has been argued that this conception of a changeable scenic picture framed by an archway was one of the principal inspirations for the later proscenium stage.

Pollux mentions other types of machinery. One is the *keraunoskopeion,* or lightning machine, which he describes as "a *periaktos* mounted high up." It has been suggested that the faces were covered with reflectors, which would revolve and flash in the sun's rays. The effectiveness of such a device, however, would depend on the position of the sun; at both Athens and Epidauros it would have been unusable for part of the performance day. Another possibility is that the faces of the *periaktoi* were painted with a continuous zig-zag pattern, which would appear to flicker as the machine revolved. Together with this went the *bronteion,* or thunder machine, consisting of a hollow vessel of earthenware or bronze full of pebbles. A late commentator mentions such a device in connection with the thunderclaps referred to in Aristophanes' *The Clouds.* Once again, however, we may doubt whether such realistic sound effects were used as early as the fifth century. Pollux also mentions, in descriptions so vague that it is impossible to reconstruct them, the *hemikyklion,* a "semicircle" (perhaps an inset scene in false perspective or miniature diorama, though Pollux locates it rather implausibly in the *orchestra*) which showed "places far from the city or persons swimming in the sea," and the *stropheion* (some sort of revolve?) which showed "persons being transformed into gods or people dying at sea or in battle." Finally, we may mention "Charon's steps," an underground entrance used for ghosts and apparitions. Only one example has been found, as part of the Hellenistic reconstruction of the Theatre of Eretria, where the tunnel leads from the *proskenion* to the center of the *orchestra*.

Thus the star performers of the Hellenistic world, who traveled from one festival to another like opera singers today and commanded salaries appropriate to an international reputation, could rely on playing in surroundings of appropriate magnificence, with the resources of an elaborate technology to support them. They could look forward to performing in the fourth-century Theatre of Megalopolis, with its capacity of, at the lowest estimate, 21,000, the largest structure of its kind in mainland Greece. Here not only the decorative facade but the entire *skene* was removable and slid away on tracks into a storehouse nearby. At Ephesus in Asia Minor, some thirty miles north of Priene, was a theatre probably begun at the end of the fourth century, and boasting an even larger capacity. Humbler performers, however, had no place at such centers. They traveled the Greek equivalent of the "straw-hat circuit" and took their theatres with them.

We may form some idea of what these portable stages were like from a group of vases of southern Italian origin, dating mostly from the first half of the fourth century. They are known as *phlyakes* vases, from the technical name for the farce performances which they portray, and show stages, actors, and costumes in considerable detail. The stages, though they vary from rudimentary to comparatively elaborate, have the same basic form which has served traveling players in all parts of the world for centuries.

The platform rests on low supporting posts, sometimes left plain, sometimes draped, and sometimes decorated like regular columns with capitals. Often a set of steps runs from the stage to

ground level, suggesting that the temporary theatres tried to reproduce, as far as possible, the features of their permanent counterparts. It is clear that some action took place on ground level
(approximating to the orchestral action of the larger theatres):
one illustration shows an obese Cheiron being helped up the steps
by two servants. The background (that is, the equivalent of the
skene) varies. Some vases indicate simple draperies, others a more
solid structure with side doors and, occasionally, windows and an
upper story. There are also indications of a roof or awning over
the acting area. That such performances were not confined to
Italy has been shown by the discovery of a similar vase dating
from the late fifth century in Attica. Here an actor dressed as Per-
seus is dancing, while at the foot of the steps sit two figures who
probably belong to the theatre's production staff. This was the
kind of theatre that, in its simplest form—trestle stage and rear
curtain—accompanied the Greek expansion overseas. Its influence
can be seen on the early Indian theatre, where the curtain behind
which the actors changed was traditionally known as *yavanika*, the
"Ionic" or "Greek" curtain. A late commentator who writes of "actors giving the effect of a city on the stage by means of curtains" is
probably referring to this type of structure. Sockets found at Syracuse and elsewhere suggest that such temporary stages could
sometimes be erected within the limits of the larger theatres.

Characterization and Masks in New Comedy

The *phlyakes* vases are still faithful in spirit to Aristophanes. They
show a collection of amiable grotesques, masked like caricatures
and wearing obscenely padded costumes, for which the basis is a
pair of tights, a close-fitting, long-sleeved undershirt, and a short
sleeveless tunic. Statuettes and replicas of masks from New Comedy, however, show that here, as we might expect, the appearance
of the characters approximated much more closely to real life. Pollux has left us a long list of such masks and makes a careful distinction between the caricatures of Old Comedy and the more
realistic effect of the New. We have the usual difficulty, however:

Pollux writes so long after the event that it is impossible to tell whether his elaborate classification was already in existence in Menander's time or emerged later on. There are, however, some obvious affinities between the list and the plays. Pollux distinguishes two old men, one with "jolly eyebrows, a full beard, lantern jaw, and dim sight, good-looking, with a pale complexion." The other is "thinner, with beady eyes, pale and morose, with a full beard, red hair, and cropped ears." We may identify the latter, perhaps, with such surly characters as Knemon in *Dyskolos*, and the former with the more amiable father from the city who arrives to put all right at the end of the play. Terence's *Adelphoe* (*The Brothers*), adapted from New Comic originals, shows a similarly contrasted pair of old men.

The list of young men in Pollux is similarly differentiated. He includes a "black" and a "delicate" young man, each suggesting a refined social upbringing: either of these would be suitable for the young Athenian suitor in *Dyskolos*, who courts Knemon's daughter and nearly comes to grief in the rugged life of the country. Contrasted to them are the "common" and "rustic" young men, the former "ruddy and athletic," the latter "weather-beaten, with broad lips, a flat nose and a shock of hair." Either of these would do for Knemon's disaffected son, who has his own poor farm near his father's. Pollux also includes the "theatening" type, the flatterer, and the parasite. The first of these is clearly a character like Polemon in Menander's *Perikeiromene*, a soldier who flies into a violent rage when he suspects his mistress of infidelity, or Pyrgopolyneices, the more broadly sketched *miles gloriosus* in Plautus' comedy of that name. Flatterers and parasites are familiar characters in New Comedy and represent a well-defined social class of adroit freeloaders who attached themselves to a wealthier citizen, offering him obsequious attendance in return for an occasional present or an invitation to a meal. Chaereas in *Dyskolos* is such a character, and surviving terracottas show what his mask must have been like. All our examples have the same general characteristics—shifty eyes, an unctuous expression, a greedy mouth, and a large nose, presumably for smelling out gifts and food, as Peniculus does at the opening of Plautus' *The Twin Menaechmi*.

Pollux continues with a long list of slave types, which broadly reduplicate the distinctions of the free-born characters, ranging from the "grandfather" to the "shaking upper slave." The latter is presumably the timorous fellow who, in Plautus, is always being drawn into plots against his will and has recently been delightfully recreated for modern audiences as Hysterium in *A Funny Thing Happened on the Way to the Forum*. Surviving terracottas of slave masks show that they were still close to the caricatures of Old Comedy, retaining the enormous mouths and eyebrows, broad nose, and wrinkled brows of the *phlyakes* paintings. In his list of women, Pollux pays most attention to whores and demimondaines, who appear more frequently in the intrigues of New Comedy than the respectable wives and mothers: in *Dyskolos*, for example, the part of Knemon's daughter, whose irresistible beauty sets the play on its complicated course, is minimal, and in Plautus and Terence the upper-class girls are usually only heard crying offstage. Pollux suggests only subtle differences between one female type and another, usually involving no more than make-up and hair style.

Although the list given by Pollux may not be applicable in every detail to the sort of comedy that Menander wrote, it clearly shares its spirit. It presents the idea of characterization by contrast. Menander's characters, like those of Plautus and Terence after him, belong to a familiar gallery of stereotypes to which the code of masks provided an easy visual key. The verbal indications of rank and character familiar in Greek tragedy are now replaced, or at least reinforced, by appeals to the eye. Pollux suggests certain conventional costume colors which must have been helpful in the large theatres: old men and young women wore white, older women blue and green, young men crimson, parasites black or grey, pimps bright colors, and rustics leather jerkins. As soon as a character walked onstage the audience could tell who he was and predict his role in the play. It is significant that when Theophrastus (371–285 B.C.) wrote his series of character studies, he made the same arbitrary distinctions that we see in the comedies, and that even Aristotle, in defining his "golden mean" in relation to character, proceeds by describing clearly differentiated extremes of each quality and suggesting that the ideal lies somewhere inbetween. Menander is traditionally described as the pupil of Theophrastus, a statement which may have been literally as well as figuratively true; and it is clear that, even in the Hellenistic world, the mask is not merely an ornament or stage necessity but a vital element of the concept of character, and hence of the theory of acting. Although Menander was lauded in the ancient world for the naturalism of his stage conceptions, modern critics have found this to be true by comparison only. Menander certainly comes closer to real life than the two-dimensional cartoon figures of Aristophanes, but the characters of New Comedy, when they change at all, do so violently and arbitrarily. Knemon's abrupt change of heart in *Dyskolos* occurs when he has fallen, offstage, into a well; in Terence's *Adelphoe* (*The Brothers*), Demea changes with alarming suddenness from his habitual surliness to smiling benignity. We look in vain for subtle modifications of character, or the progressive transitions on which the modern actor builds his performance. Although the individual personality of the actor was now much more widely recognized, the mask still had its effect, imposing itself upon the characterization of the role, importing its own behavioral associations, and restricting the performer to the limited range of language and action appropriate to the stereotype. The abrupt changes of character that do occur convey the effect of taking off one mask and putting on another.

CHAPTER FOUR

The Roman Theatre: From the Beginnings to the Early Empire

Origins of the Roman Theatre

The earliest Italian drama of which we have any knowledge came from the region of Campania, in the southern half of the peninsula. It was particularly associated with the town of Atella—hence the name *fabula Atellana,* or Atellan farce—and was originally performed in Oscan, the language of that region. Later earning popularity in Rome, it was translated into Latin, the language of the dominant city. The original performances must have been largely, if not entirely, unscripted, using stock characters in variations on a few basic plots. Called by some scholars "the Italian Punch and Judy," it suggests a cruder prototype of the later Italian *commedia dell'arte*, with the emphasis on visual humor and broadly drawn, familiar characterizations. Most of our information comes at second hand, deriving from later, more sophisticated writers, who went slumming for their material and gave the farces a temporary vogue in literary circles. Among the great, unlettered mass of the Italian public, their popularity endured for centuries: Atellan performances are in evidence in Petronius' fictional account of Trimalchio's feast, set in the reign of Nero. But we depend for our knowledge of the arts in Rome mainly on the tastes of the educated minority, and such popular forms are rarely even mentioned.

We know at least the names of some of the principal characters, which prefigure some of the basic types of the later *commedia*. Maccus was the bumbling antihero, an oafish figure who could do nothing right. The full name of the third-century playwright, Titus Maccius (or Maccus) Plautus, suggests a connection with this early rustic acting tradition: the traditional *Life* states that Plautus was working in the theatre for some time before he turned to authorship. Pappus, the Latin equivalent of the Greek *pappos*, grandfather, was the comic old man. Dossennus was perhaps a hunchback; his name suggests a connection with the Latin *dorsum*, "back." Bucco was perhaps a fat-faced character (cf. Latin *bucca*, "cheek," whence derive Italian *bocca* and French *bouche*). The name of Manducus, described as an ogre-like figure with champing jaws, is more certainly related to the vernacular *manducare*, "chew," "eat" (cf. Italian *mangiare*, French *manger*). It must be emphasized that these etymologies are only conjectural. If correct, however, they suggest that the early players may have worn masks, as the *phylakes* actors in southern Italy certainly did. This becomes important to the vexed question of the use of the mask by Plautus and Terence. The existence of Atellan masks is perhaps supported by the popularity of identical twin plays, as we know from such titles as *The Twin Macci*, or *The Two Dossenni*: the availability of masks tends, as in the Greek New Comedy, to be productive of this type of plot. Of the stage on which these actors performed, if any, we know nothing.

The true history of the Roman theatre, as the Roman historians themselves recognized, began in contacts with other powers: first the Etruscans, the mysterious people to the north, whose history was bound up with that of the emergent city, and later the thriving Greek colonies in southern Italy. It was the Etruscans who, prior to the foundation of the Republic, supplied Rome with the last three of her traditional list of kings. The Romans, who derived a number of their important institutions from the Etruscans, credited them with having introduced a form of music and dance spectacle into the city. Tradition dated this in 364 B.C., a plague year, when Etruscan performers were brought in as a last resort to appease the anger of the gods. Such a dance scene is portrayed on a mural from the *Tomba del Triclinio* at Tarquinia, which shows a musician with a double flute, one male, and two female dancers. The Augustan historian Livy and Valerius Maximus, who wrote another antiquarian treatise somewhat later, tell substantially the same story, suggesting a common source. Valerius Maximus' account, which is the shorter, reads as follows:

This matter [*i.e.*, the plague] provided a reason for importing a performer [*ludius*] from Etruria, whose grace and agility in his art—skills traditionally derived from the Curetes and Lydians, from whom the Etruscans traced their origins—refreshed and delighted Roman eyes with their novelty. Since the Etruscan for stage performer was *histrio*, that word was adopted for the Roman actor.

Livy, who agrees with this derivation, stresses that the original performance was primarily balletic, "without any singing, without even imitating the action of singers," but involving "not ungraceful evolutions in the Tuscan fashion." Words came later, a rough libretto, derived from the local verse tradition and adapted to Etruscan music.

Roman tradition also ascribed to the Etruscans cruder entertainments, the combats later to become fashionable as the gladiatorial games. These too are illustrated in Etruscan tomb paintings. A well-known mural from the *Tomba degli Auguri* at Tarquinia shows a wrestling match keenly watched by a figure who may either be spectator or umpire, and a man with his head in a sack being attacked by a mastiff. A cryptic figure, perhaps wearing a mask, is seen at one point urging the dog on, and at another running away. He is labeled *phersu*, which may be the equivalent of the Latin *persona* ("mask"). Another mural, from the *Tomba delle Bighe*, also at Tarquinia, shows a chariot race watched by a noisily conversational crowd in grandstands. These things, however, look forward to a later era of Roman entertainment: for the moment, we are concerned with the drama proper.

Livius Andronicus: Writer and Actor

Out of the loose amalgamation of song, dance, and the spoken word, which Livy calls *saturae* ("medleys"), came the play. The Romans found their own Thespis in Livius Andronicus, supposedly a Greek captured by their armies at the siege of Tarentum, the only colony founded by the Spartans and one of the most important Greek cities in southern Italy. Livius is certainly a more solid historical figure than his Greek counterpart. We have two firm dates for his career: 240 B.C., when he brought the first Greek drama, in Latin translation, to Rome and 207, when, during the second war with Carthage, he was commissioned by the religious authorities to compose a hymn to be sung through the city by twenty-seven maidens. Its purpose was to allay public despondency caused by a series of bad omens. He probably died shortly afterward, for when another hymn was called for seven years later, it was entrusted to another composer.

Roman tradition typically attributed to native benevolence Livius' rapid rise from prisoner-of-war to poet laureate. He was said to have entered the house of Lucius Livius as a slave, to have been freed in recognition of his talents, and to have gone on to compose important translations from the Greek poets still in use centuries later, as well as being the father of Roman drama. His version of the *Odyssey* was still a school book in Horace's time. The story is unfortunately suspect. It is told with minor variations of several other literary figures (in Roman drama, for instance, of Caecilius Statius and Terence), and we must doubt whether it was true in every case. The dates are also difficult to reconcile with known historical events. Tarentum was captured twice by the Romans, once in 272 and again in 209 B.C. Neither of these dates is satisfactory for the arrival of Livius in Rome. If the earlier is meant, Livius must have been extremely young at the time, for we know he was still alive in 207, writing his hymn. Where then could he have acquired the knowledge of Greek literature and drama that the tradition presupposes? And if he did not come until 209, how could he have been performing Greek drama in Rome over thirty years earlier? We obviously have here a simplified story of what must have been a long and complex process of transmission, hung onto a convenient name. Ancient historians loved to personalize, and Livy, who tells us the story, had a particular reason for doing so, for the man who traditionally set Livius Andronicus free was one of his own forebears. We can say at least that the Greek influence was recognized as dominant, and that, as in Greece itself, the drama emerged from, or was grafted onto, festivals which had no previous theatrical content.

Livius Andronicus the writer belongs to the history of Latin literature. Livius the actor, however, is another matter, and there is another story about him which throws an interesting light on Roman theatrical practice. In the early period, at least, the Roman playwright, like his Greek predecessors, seems to have been a jack-of-all-trades. Livius is said to have acted so extensively in his own productions that he strained his voice and was compelled, with the indulgence of the audience, to use a boy to sing the musical portions of the play, while he mimed the action. There are two possible inferences from this story. One is that the actor relied heavily on gesture (recalling Livy's emphasis on the balletic quality of the Etruscan performance); the other, that music was an important factor in the Roman plays from the start. It continued to be so; and it is worth anticipating the chronological sequence to see how vital music remained to the concept of drama.

The Musical Element in Roman Theatre

In fifth-century Greece, as we have seen, the musical element was chiefly the responsibility of the chorus. There were still choruses in Roman tragedy, but comedy, which early established itself as the only true popular form, almost entirely eliminated them. We may see their vestigial remains in one play of Plautus, *Rudens* (*The Rope*), where a group of fishermen make a brief entrance, sing of the miseries of their trade, submit to questions from one of the principals, and promptly depart. This musical loss, however, was compensated for in other ways. The actors were called upon to deliver complex lyric passages, known as *cantica* ("sung portions") to distinguish them from *diverbia* ("spoken dialogue"). Already obvious from the meter, the distinction is usually made additionally clear in our texts by the marginal notations C or DV. The form of Roman comedy, therefore, has justly been compared to that of Gilbert and Sullivan operetta, being composed of substantial dialogue scenes interspersed with frequent, and often irrelevant, song.

We see from the comedies of Plautus how extensive this compensation could be. They are metrically much more flexible than the fragments of Greek New Comedy that we know. The greater part of Menander's *Dyskolos* is written in iambic trimeter, though Knemon's long speech in the fourth episode was a more ponderous meter which may have had musical accompaniment. The same may have been true of the play's conclusion, where a stage direction calls for flute music. But Plautus and the other comic writers seem to have adapted meters at will, introducing a greater lyric content. The same is clearly true of tragedy in those cases where we can compare the Roman adaptations with the Greek originals. It has been argued with some probability that the Roman playwrights were here following an acting rather than a literary tradition and embodying in their versions songs, dances, and musical flourishes that the Hellenistic actors, who had no respect for the text, had included in their own performances.

Music was provided by flutes. In some cases we know the names of the artists from the *didaskalia,* or production information, prefaced to the manuscript of the play. For all the plays of Terence, for example, we are told that the accompaniment was furnished by Flaccus, slave of Claudius, and composed for the "equal *tibiae,*" that is, two pipes of equal length capable of being played simultaneously. For the extent to which *cantica* were employed, we may look at Plautus' *The Twin Menaechmi,* which has five: a song of curses sung by a husband to his nagging wife, a prostitute's musical soliloquy on the mysteries of her trade, the husband's song about the tiresome duties of a citizen, a lament on age by the comic old man, and a slave's complaint. It is interesting to note that, here as elsewhere, the *cantica* tend to occur after what television would now call "natural breaks in the action," corresponding roughly (though not invariably) with the act divisions inserted by later editors. The original performances were probably played without intermission, but the *cantica* fulfill at least one function of the Greek choruses in providing a periodic relaxation by means of music and dance. In Plautus' *Pseudolus,* we have a rare case of a musician entertaining the audience alone while the stage is left empty. The conniving slave who gives the play its title announces that he has to go inside to work out a plan: "I'm off now, but I won't keep you long. This flute player will amuse you till I get back." Sometimes music and songs of a specific type are worked plausibly into the action, as in *Casina,* which has a wedding song with flute accompaniment, *Curculio,* where a lovesick boy serenades a closed door, and *Stichus,* where music accompanies a drinking bout. At such moments we may suppose that, as in Shakespeare's theatre, the regular musicians were brought onstage as characters.

Holidays and Festivals

Once the drama had won acceptance at Rome, its performance was associated, as in Greece, with important public holidays and religious festivals. The Latin word *ludi* can mean both plays and

the festive occasions at which they were performed. In the Republic, these festivals were five in number. The *ludi Megalenses,* or
Megalesian games, were held in early April in honor of the goddess Cybele, or "Great Mother," imported from Asia Minor during
the Carthaginian Wars. Established in 191 B.C., the festival offered
perhaps as many as six days of dramatic performances. Cybele's
temple stood on the Palatine, Rome's most solemn hill, and the
plays seem to have been given in the precincts, with the statue
of the goddess looking on as that of Dionysos had done in his
theatre shrine in Athens. Some plays were specifically related to
the cult of Cybele and her eunuch acolyte Attis, but others were
of more general interest: Plautus' *Pseudolus* was performed at the
dedication. Livy, quoting earlier authority, tells us that this was
the first such ceremony to involve plays. Some works of Terence
were given here in later years.

In late April came the *ludi Florales* (Floral Games) in front of
Flora's temple on the Aventine Hill, and in July the games in
honor of Apollo. This festival was inaugurated in 212 B.C., but
plays were probably not introduced until some time later. Sep-
tember brought the Roman Games, *ludi Romani,* the most important festival of all, and traditionally founded by Romulus. These
games provide another Greek parallel, for they seem to have been
associated, at least originally, with Liber, the Roman equivalent
of Dionysos. The Christian polemicist Tertullian, centuries later,
was to sneer at the theatre as "the home of Venus and Liber,"
both gods of carnal pleasures. The nondramatic part of these
games took place in the Circus Maximus, whose outline can still
be seen in the valley between the Aventine and Palatine hills.
Where the plays were given is not clear. Finally, in November,
came the Plebeian Games, *ludi Plebeii.* These were founded some
time in the later third century, and held in the Circus Flaminius,
built on marshy ground further up the Tiber.

It is evident that the opportunities for theatre-going in Rome
rapidly increased, and that the actor, although ostensibly restricted to festival performances, had far greater scope to exercise

his profession. As the entertainments were often used as vote-catching devices and sponsored by incumbent magistrates or candidates for office, there was every inducement to extend the number of performances. Outside the established festivals, plays could also be given at the dedication of new temples (we know, for instance, of contracts let out for theatres in 179 and 174 B.C.) and at more private occasions. Plays were a familiar feature of funeral games. Terence's *The Mother-in-Law* and *The Brothers* were given at the funeral of Lucius Aemilius Scaurus in 160 B.C. It is important, therefore, to see the plays not as isolated occurrences but as part of a wider complex of festival activity, in which playwrights had to compete with other fare for the public attention. We have some sense of this from the fast-talking, wise-cracking prologues of Plautus, which suggest the patter of a side-show barker catching his audience on the wing; we see it even more clearly in Terence's complaints about audiences who deserted his delicate comedies for tight-rope walkers and gymnasts.

These festival associations, unfortunately, did not impart to the Roman theatre the dignity that the art had enjoyed in Greece. Some of the early practitioners enjoyed considerable prestige, as the history of Livius Andronicus shows. His hymn for the year 207 was so successful that a Temple of Minerva on the Aventine was dedicated in his honor and formed the center of a college of playwrights and actors. Quintus Ennius, a later playwright of repute, who was born the year after Livius made his first contribution to the festival, took up residence in the same district. But, as in the later Greek theatre, professionalism carried its stigma. Livy, in his account of the early days, makes a sharp distinction between professionals and amateurs, telling us that the gilded youth of Rome abandoned the acting of comedies to the professionals and revived the older tradition of the Atellan farces, not letting them be "polluted" (significant word) by the professionals. "That is why" he continues, "the performers of the Atellan plays retain their civic rights, and serve in the army as if they had no connection with the stage." The professional actor, then, could expect at least partial disenfranchisement, and, as a member of an increasingly odious profession, hostility from the puritanical element in the Roman Senate.

Theatre Architecture and Stage Equipment

For the structure of the early theatre and its mechanical equipment we must look largely to the plays themselves. Archaeology cannot help us, for there was no permanent theatre in Rome until the declining years of the Republic. Our evidence consists of twenty complete and one fragmentary comedy by Plautus and six by Terence. The fragments of tragedies and comedies by other writers offer little assistance. We have enough, however, to determine the general nature of the settings required; and our evidence suggests that all the plays we know could be fitted into the framework provided by the Hellenistic stage or its portable equivalent, the rudimentary platform used for the *phlyakes* farces. It is no accident that the beginnings of Roman drama coincide with the first Roman involvement with major foreign powers. The wars of expansion which took Roman troops to the Greek colonies in southern Italy and Sicily, long a stronghold of Greek culture, also introduced them to a fully developed theatre. It was natural that the Romans should absorb, along with Greek plots, the structures in which those plots were given life.

The surviving comedies can be performed, without exception, against the standard Hellenistic facade, with its architectural decoration and three doors. In most cases, this all-purpose background (Latin *scaena* or *frons scaenae*) is given a precise location by the Prologue, in language which makes it clear that the audience could expect no visual differentiation from one play to another. Thus the Prologue to *The Twin Menaechmi* tells us that he can go from here to Epidamnus without moving from the spot; and, later, that "this is Epidamnus, for the duration of the play." In *Truculentus* we are told that Plautus wished to create Athens "without benefit of architect," and that "this stage is Athens, while we act our comedy." The argument as to whether Plautus actually wrote these prologues himself is here irrelevant: their expository purpose is the same. Often the Prologue goes on to identify the three doors with their inhabitants. If not, this is generally obvious from the ensuing action. Thus, in *The Twin Menaechmi,* one door represents the house of Menaechmus of Epidamnus, one that of the prostitute Erotium, and the third, perhaps, that of the Doctor, who is summoned later in the play. *The Pot of Gold* requires a house for Euclio, another for his millionaire neighbor Megadorus, and the Temple of Faith, in which the miser conceals his beloved treasure. In some plays, as in the Greek New Comedy, only two doors are needed: thus *Mostellaria* (*The Haunted House*) which requires houses for Theoropides and Simo, and *The Rope,* where we see the cottage of Daemones and the shrine of Venus. In *The Haunted House* there is talk of the pillars at the vestibule of Simo's house, which are described as needing another coat of tar. This, of course, tells us nothing about the construction of the *scaena.* The columns may simply have been part of the painted background, or left to the audience's imagination.

There are several cases where one of the doors represents a temple or shrine. Two examples have been noted above; another occurs in *Curculio,* where we are told that "this is the shrine of Aesculapius" and, later, "this is the altar of Venus before the doors." It is clear that the stage altar was still a permanent fixture, ready to be used when needed, or at least a highly familiar property. In *The Pot of Gold,* Lyconides' slave sits on the altar to overhear the miser plotting to bury his treasure, and *The Haunted House* concludes with a hilarious scene, where Tranio, the peccant slave, seeks sanctuary by squatting on the altar and refuses to move until he has been forgiven. Similarly in *The Rope,* the maidens in distress run to the altar of Venus for safety. This use of the shrine-altar complex recalls the theory noted in Chapter One, and again in connection with New Comedy, that the shrine originally served as the informing image for the *skene.* In Rome it is even possible (though not likely) that, as the connection between the early performances and religious festivals is evident, some portion of the actual temple facade may have been used.

That the scene-building, at least occasionally, used an upper story is evident from *Amphitruo*, a mistaken-identity comedy in which Jupiter disguises himself as the warrior Amphitruo to seduce the latter's wife, and Mercury compounds the deception by assuming the likeness of Amphitruo's slave Sosias. At one point Mercury, seeing Amphitruo approaching, announces that he will go up to the roof (*dein susum ascendere in tectum*) and mock him. Amphitruo arrives to find the doors locked in his face, and an angry shouting scene ensues. At the end of the play, Jupiter appears with a clap of thunder to deliver his explanation and benediction and announces that he will return to heaven (*ego in caelum migro*). It is tempting to suppose that he too appears on the roof, and that the closing appeal for applause "for the sake of Jupiter in the highest" (*Iovi' summi caussa clare plaudite*) is in comic recognition of this fact. We may recall here a *phlyakes* painting which shows similar requirements for an earlier Greek farce version of the same story. Amphitruo's wife, a much more willing victim than in Plautus, is shown appearing seductively at an upper window; Zeus-Jupiter, crowned, approaches the window with a ladder; and Hermes-Mercury, with wide-brimmed hat and traditional staff, holds a lantern to light his way. In Plautus' *Miles Gloriosus* there is much talk of peering down skylights and chasing on the roof, but none of the action need be visible. In *The Rope*, the constellation Arcturus, who speaks the Prologue, refers to the damage caused by the recent storm to Daemones' tiles: this may indicate that he too is on the roof and making a comic reference to his own precarious position.

The quarrel between Amphitruo and Mercury is of particular interest for the possible light it sheds on tragic practice, about which we are otherwise largely uninformed. *Amphitruo*, unique in Roman comedy in involving major deities as characters, may have been offered as deliberate parody of a tragedy fresh in the memory of the audience. Mercury announces in the Prologue that this is not the first time Jupiter has appeared on the stage. He has been seen in tragedy and "last year, when the actors on this very stage called upon Jupiter, he came and helped them out." The slave Sceparnio at the beginning of *The Rope*, which was probably written about the same time, refers to the recent storm as "no mere wind, but like Alcumena in Euripides." It has been suggested, therefore, that both these references are to the same play, and that the audience of the previous year had seen a tragedy involving both Alcumena (the Greek Alkmene) and a storm, adapted from the Greek—possibly an *Alcumena* by Ennius, who was popular at the time, or by Pacuvius.

The version of the story used is suggested by two vase paintings from the third quarter of the fourth century, showing the efforts of Amphitryon to burn Alkmene alive as punishment for her unwilling infidelity. Alkmene is on a pyre, which is being ignited by a torch. Overhead, two goddesses, with a rainbow, are pouring rain on the flames, while Zeus stands by. (We may compare the scene in *The Rope* where the pimp Labrax calls for wood to burn his victims alive on the altar, and, earlier, a fragment from Menander's *Perinthia*, where the same treatment is proposed for a slave sitting on the altar in supplication: both are reminiscent of Lycus' threats to Heracles' family in *The Madness of Heracles*.) There is every probability, then, that *Amphitruo* is burlesquing effects familiar from tragedy, in a manner reminiscent of the *phlyakes* parodies and of Aristophanes himself. When Mercury mocks Amphitruo from the roof, he seems to pour a bucket of water on his head (though the text is very corrupt at this point), and Amphitruo is eventually stupefied by the thunder-clap of Jupiter. We may conjecture that, even so early, Roman adaptations of Greek tragedy were tending toward the spectacular.

This is supported by hints of "flying machinery" in the tragic fragments, and an equivalent of the Charonian steps, for the appearance of ghosts. Cicero, who apparently saw a revival of *Iliona*, by Pacuvius, in the first century, notes that the ghost of Deiphilus appeared to the heroine to the accompaniment of soft music, and apparently from underground. His first words were "I call you, mother," and Cicero quotes them again in a story about

Appius Claudius Pulcher, which is a clear reference to tragic practice: "He used to come every day to watch the gladiatorial shows,
but was never seen arriving. Making his way furtively under the
planks, he used to pop up suddenly, as if about to say 'I call you,
mother!' " It is probable that the original productions also used the
hollow space under the stage to bring up ghosts through trap-
doors.

In Roman comedy, as we have seen, the stage almost invariably represents a street, and the stage doors the houses fronting
on it. The combination of *scaena, proscaenium* and stage altar
provided an all-purpose background suitable for any play. There
are some possible references to statues on stage; one, in a fragment of Plautus' *Boeotia,* to a sundial (possibly represented by
the stage altar) and one in the *Asinaria* to a descent down a slope.
The actors may still have been using the ground level for some
scenes, with steps ascending to the stage in the *phlyakes* manner.

Theatre of Ostia Antica,
set for a modern revival of Plautus' *Pseudolus.*
[Courtesy of the Italian Government Travel Office]

Even for those plays which required a rustic setting, the standard background could have been used with the minimum of adaptation or imagination. In the fragmentary *Vidularia*, we are told that "this is the myrtle-grove of Venus"; perhaps one of the doors was simply left open here, to suggest an open space. *The Rope* is set on the seashore, where Sceparnio is seen "digging" as the play opens. Later in the play the fisherman Gripus enters, chuckling over his lucky catch. He has hauled up a chest which will turn out to contain the tokens identifying the benighted, shipwrecked maidens and free them from the pursuing brothel keeper. The action suggests that we do not immediately see the chest; and Gripus may well enter with one end of the net, leaving the other offstage—perhaps through the unused third door, left open to suggest open country—to be hauled into sight later on.

There is no need to assert, as several literal-minded scholars have done, that the basic setting involved alleys, embrasures, or other places of concealment to allow for the frequent scenes in which one character must be unobserved by another, or make remarks that the other is supposed not to be able to overhear, developing two separate and mutually oblivious patterns of action independently. Examples occur in *Amphitruo*, where Mercury and Sosias talk about each other to themselves and to the audience, but are apparently unaware of each other's presence; *The Two Bacchises*, where Cleomachus seems to be oblivious of the other people on the stage; and the long scene in *The Haunted House*, where Philolaches spies on Philematium at her toilette and delivers a sardonic running commentary without her hearing a word. Such scenes, however, permit no conclusions about theatre architecture, or even about the size of the stage. The convention of invisibility, or inaudibility, is one of the easiest to establish, particularly in such plays as these, where reality is kept at arm's length. It may be relevant that later paintings relating to theatrical scenes tend to show the characters facing front, perhaps indicating the conventional blocking.

But in most ways the setting is taken very literally indeed; and we may see in the Roman stage the continuation of the Hellenistic tendency for the scene to impose its presence on the actors. The stage (*proscaenium*) represents the street, and every effort is made to provide plausible motivation for carrying the action "outdoors." Obviously, the playwrights are aided by the fact of writing for a Mediterranean society, where much happens in the open air that in colder climates tends to take place within four walls. Even so, it is a little strange to find a fashionable harlot bringing out her make-up table into the street, and scenes of plotting occurring in the open when they might more reasonably take place inside. The playwright's anxiety to justify such breaches of probability shows how much of the old freedom of the presentational theatre had been lost. In another sense, too, the setting dominates the action; in this sort of comedy, the doors are as important as in French bedroom farce, and we are often watching them as much as we are watching the characters onstage, to see which will open next, and who will emerge. This is particularly evident, for instance, in the sequence of thefts and misunderstandings in *The Pot of Gold*, when one door is opening just as another closes, and characters miss each other by a hairbreadth. Our attention is drawn to them by the repeated tag "the door's opening, someone's coming out," one of the most familiar lines in Roman comedy.

Relation of Audience to the Play

The extrovert and uninhibited comedy of Plautus tells us a good deal about the nature of the audience, and shows that the fairground atmosphere of early Roman comedy had restored much of the old communion between players and public that the Hellenistic drama had lost. From the prologues, particularly that of *Pseudolus*, we can assemble a composite picture of a jolly, raucous holiday crowd whose attention could easily be diverted. They sat on benches in the auditorium (*cavea*) where they could sit, and stood when they could not, with ushers to show them to their seats and a herald whose bellows called them to order. Tacitus, writing under the Empire, affects to believe that the early theatre had no seats, but the Plautine Prologues show this to be untrue;

Tacitus, as is his wont, idealizes the supposed austerity of an earlier Rome. The Prologue of *Pseudolus* gradually makes himself heard above the hubbub:

I don't want any worn-out old whore sitting on the stage; I don't want to hear a murmur from the lictor and his rods; I don't want the usher blocking anybody's view, or showing people to their seats while the actors are on. Keep awake, if you can. Slaves, don't sit down, leave the seats for the free men. Nurses, don't bring little kids in here, they make too much noise. And you women, don't gossip or laugh too loud. And don't forget the bake-shop's open outside; send your servants for tarts while they're piping hot.

He was probably receiving a commission from the stall next door.

The audience was clearly a cross-section of the working-class community, farmers, small shopkeepers, and, particularly, soldiers, for Plautus wrote when Rome was at war. Mercury, in the Prologue to *Amphitruo,* appeals for favor as the god his audience worships in their businesses; in *Captivi* (*Prisoners of War*) the spectators are characterized as "the most impartial judges at home, and the finest soldiers in time of war"; in *Asinaria,* when the audience has been invited to sit down—"only take care you pay first"—Mars, the war god, is called upon to bless them. In such circumstances, with the soldiers back from the front and the civilians enjoying a respite from workaday drudgery, drinking, laughing, and chatting, it is not surprising that it was difficult to hear. Thus in *Prisoners of War,* the Prologue breaks off his exposition to answer a real or imagined objection from some poor sufferer at the back of the house: "Got that? Fine! The man at the back says he hasn't. Come up front, then. Nowhere to sit? Well, you've got two legs, haven't you? I'm not about to rupture myself on your account." From *Amphitruo,* we learn of the existence of organized claques; from the petulant prologues of Terence we hear what could happen when an audience turned vicious.

The rapport established by the prologue spills over into the play. Plautine characters acknowledge the presence of the audience and invite their attention and complicity. In *Curculio,* one of the backstage staff interrupts the action with an irrelevant monologue, a scurrilous guide to the topography of Rome. In *The Haunted House*, Philolaches, in the middle of his cynical comments about women, turns to the audience and says, "Any of you who have old wives at home will know what I'm talking about"; while the slave Tranio, fearing a beating, frantically tries to hire one of the spectators to take his place. In *Cistellaria* (*The Casket Comedy*), a distressed Halisca asks the audience for help in finding the lost casket. The same device is used in *The Pot of Gold*, when Euclio, almost out of his mind with despair, demands to know the whereabouts of his vanished treasure:

> I beg, I pray you, I beseech you, come
> To my assistance, tell me where he went,
> The man who stole it—You, sir, what do you say?
> I'm sure you can be trusted; you have an honest face.
> What is it? What's so funny? I know your lot—
> Crooks, that's what you are, ninety-nine percent of you.
> You sit in whitewashed togas, and pretend
> That you're respectable—doesn't anyone here have it?
> You don't know? Murder! Then tell me who does!
> Don't you know anything?
>
> [vv. 715 ff.]

Sometimes the reverse effect is sought. In *The Haunted House*, a slave running from punishment appeals to the audience not to give him away. In *The Twin Menaechmi* the bewildered husband, suspected of insanity, flees his pursuers with a parting aside, "Don't tell the old man where I've gone!" And, finally, there are cases which may actually involve entrances through the crowd, with the actors cursing those who get in their path. This may, however, represent no more than the typical braggadocio of the comic slave in a hurry. But there are sufficient examples to show that the audience was engaged in the action, by word or gesture, from the Prologue to the final, obligatory appeal for applause, as if the playwright, once having caught their attention, was afraid of what might happen if he let them go.

Terence, obviously, was not afraid to let go. He counted on the play to keep the audience's attention. Even his Prologues are directed, not so much at the spectators, as at the poetasters of his time. His plays assume a prepared and attentive audience, who had read the originals in Greek and needed no humoring or assistance. His black humor when the public walked out on him shows how wrong he was. But Terence, however much he might have hoped for general recognition, was writing primarily for a coterie audience, the forerunners of those who listened to the closet dramas of Seneca. For this reason his plays are, in every sense, closer to the Greek; his characters move in a self-contained world, constructed with meticulous detail, and betray no awareness of the audience's presence.

Plautus' plays also contain several in-jokes, fragments of backstage gossip that give us a glimpse of how the companies worked. As we have already seen, the actors were second-class citizens. Even if they were not all slaves, as was once thought, their condition was little better. In the Epilogue of *The Casket Comedy,* an actor steps out of character to make a wry joke about his expectations: "anyone who's made a mistake will be thrashed; anyone who hasn't will be given a drink." It has been well pointed out that, even if this is not intended to be taken literally, it would be difficult to imagine such a joke being made about the actors in the Theatre of Dionysos. The troupe was known collectively as the *grex,* a word used elsewhere of a flock of sheep, and led by the actor-manager, the *dominus.* We know two of the latter by name. Titus Publilius Pellio staged some of Plautus' plays, though the author seems to have fallen out with him by the time *The Two Bacchises* was written. There he has a character say, "I love *Epidicus* with my own life; but there's no show I hate to watch more, if Pellio is playing in it." Lucius Ambivius Turpio staged all six comedies of Terence. In the second Prologue to *The Mother-in-Law,* he announces that he is staking his own prestige on a revival of a play which had already failed twice, as he had earlier used his talents to bring Caecilius Statius, Terence's predecessor, the recognition he deserved. The company was probably kept as small as possible for reasons of economy. There is evidence of doubling in *The Boy from Carthage,* where the Prologue announces, "I'll go and put on my costume now," and, a few lines later, "I'm going now. I want to turn myself into somebody else." With maximum doubling, Plautus' *The Casket Comedy* and *Stichus* could be given by three actors, though *The Boy from Carthage* and *The Rope* need at least six, and *Trinummus* probably more. Terence needs a minimum of five. Though the principals might double, there are scenes in the plays which require numerous extras, probably provided by cheap slave labor drawn from the backstage personnel. In *The Pot of Gold* we have a procession of slaves and music-girls, arriving to provide the wedding feast: there are similar scenes in *The Two Bacchises* and *Truculentus*. In *The Twin Menaechmi*, the visiting Menaechmus and his slave Messenio are accompanied by other slaves with luggage. A procession of slaves appears in *Pseudolus*, being beaten as they shuffle out to receive their orders for the day. Several plays need "trusties," the slave-overseers who were put in charge of their fellows. A passing reference in the Prologue to *Prisoners of War* indicates the amount of crowd spectacle to be expected in contemporary tragedy. It is announced that, although the play is set in wartime, all the battles will take place offstage "because it isn't fair for us to attempt impromptu tragedy when we're only fitted out for comedy." The inference is that the tragic stage was already addicted to the mass spectacle familiar from the Hellenistic performances and ridiculed later by Horace in the theater of the early Empire.

Costumes

For the plays that we have, the actors wore Greek dress, in accordance with the supposed location. For men, this consisted of tunic (Greek *chiton,* Latin *tunica*) and mantle (Greek *himation,* Latin *pallium* or *palla*): hence the term *comoedia palliata* for Latin adaptations of Greek comedy, as opposed to *comoedia togata,* comedy in a Roman setting. The *pallium,* draped in various ways, was particularly useful to the actor, for it could help him suggest a mood. References in the plays indicate a recognized costume code: the mantle trailing on the ground indicates sorrow, while the "running slave" entering on urgent business hitches his *pallium* around him to leave his body clear for action. Characters entering a temple or shrine customarily throw their *pallia* over their heads in accordance with normal Roman practice.

Some special types of costume are called for. Ghosts in tragedy wore the shabby dress of mourning. Pseudolus, about to disguise himself as a messenger, calls for a *chlamys* and *petasus*. The *chlamys* was the shorter cloak commonly worn by military men (and also, according to Horace, by the tragic chorus); the *petasus* was the wide-brimmed hat. This suggests the costume of Hermes-Mercury on the *phlyakes* vase (see p. 104) and probably in *Amphitruo* also. In *The Boy from Carthage,* the costume of the traveling salesman must be distinctively Carthaginian to provoke so many jokes; his slaves have rings in their noses. A foreign costume also seems likely for the sycophant in *Trinummus.* Wreaths are worn as signs of celebration and staffs carried to indicate authority or old age. Women wore the same basic combination, though the *tunica* was longer, extending almost to the ground: it was caught around the body twice, by the *strophium,* or girdle, under the breasts and a cord around the waist. We may assume that the conventional colors listed by Pollux still applied.

Theatre Personnel and the Playwright

The costumes were the responsibility of the *choragus*—the Romans used the Greek word, in a less dignified sense—who may have been a permanent member of the company or an independent agent working in conjunction with the magistrates who sponsored the shows. The latter is suggested by his appearance as a character in *Curculio,* wondering whether he will ever get back the costume he rented (though this is not conclusive; the possessive wardrobe mistress is not unknown in our day). In *Persa,* Saturio is told to disguise himself as a foreigner and find the same costume for his daughter. When he asks where he can get them, he is told, "Pick them up from the *choragus.* He ought to give them; the *aediles* [magistrates responsible for the games] rented them out [or contracted for them, *locaverunt*] to be used." The noun *choragia* embraces stage equipment of all sorts, and the *choragus* was presumably also responsible for the enormous quantity of props used in the comedies. Most of these are ordinary domestic furniture, couches, dressing tables, mirrors, jewelboxes, chests, perfume bottles, jugs and basins, pots and pans, fetters for slaves, food—some of it perhaps still on the hoof, as in *The Pot of Gold,* where lambs are brought in for the banquet. Lupine seeds were used for stage money—"comic gold," as one character calls it.

Among the other theatre personnel, we have already noted the slave-musicians. Flaccus, the slave of Claudius, was responsible for the music for all Terence's plays. The production information (*didaskalia*) for Plautus' *Stichus* lists Oppius Marcipor in the same function: *por* is *puer* ("slave"). There were other officials called the *conductores,* whose function remains unclear. In one prologue Plautus utters the pious hope that the play will go well "for the sake of the *grex,* the *domini,* and the *conductores.*" This implies that they had a financial interest in the performance and may have been the money-takers or the *aediles* themselves, in their function as producers.

It has already been stressed that the Roman theatre was a wholly commercial enterprise. The playwright's connection with the company was now limited to providing material on a cash basis. He was at the mercy of the public and the companies who employed him, as the traditional life of Plautus shows. He is said to have begun his career as a working member of a theatrical troupe (as stage carpenter or, perhaps, actor, as his retention of the old stage name Maccus would indicate) but to have lost his savings in speculations. Reduced to working in a flour mill, one of the lowest forms of labor and looked on with horror even by slaves, he found time to write the plays that were eventually to make him famous. The twenty-one comedies, variations on a few basic formulas, show how the playwright was forced to place output above originality. Sold outright for a lump sum, the play passed out of the author's control; there were no royalties, no residuals, even though popular hits were frequently revived. The Prologue to *Casina*, obviously not by Plautus himself, testifies to the popularity of old plays in general and offers the present performance as a revival of a work "which the older among you will remember . . . and which walked off with all the honors on its first appearance." A successful author could not even call his name his own. Plautus was a guaranteed box-office draw, and unscrupulous managers did not hesitate to advertise other men's work as his. Terence's position in the theatre was an exception to the general rule. We know, on his own admission, that he had patrons, though we do not know exactly who they were; it was presumably their financial support that gave him the dangerous freedom to write as he liked and made possible the dogged revival of *Hecyra* (*The Mother-in-Law*), a proven failure. Ambivius Turpio, however, in the second Prologue to that play, announces that he is staging it at his own expense. A late source attributes some financial success to Terence, noting that his *Eunuchus* (*The Eunuch*) was sold for 6,000 sesterces. This enormous sum, however, must remain suspect.

Stage Building

Despite—or perhaps because of—the popularity of the theatre, it was a long while before Rome boasted a permanent stage building. A series of attempts to establish one was defeated by senatorial opposition: throughout the history of the Republic there ran a streak of rugged puritanism which saw Greek influence in general, and plays in particular, as morally destructive, and refused to give them a permanent home. The festival theatres, erected for the most part in the circuses and utilizing the existing seating had to be taken down, of course, when the plays were over; but the authorities were equally stern in insisting on the removal of theatres in other parts of the city, which used their own wooden bleachers. In 155 B.C., not long after the death of Terence, work was started on a stone theatre with permanent seats. The next year the Senate suffered a change of heart and ordered the structure to be demolished. Temporary theatres, however, continued to be built on an increasingly magnificent scale. We know of one for the triumphal shows given by Mummius when he returned from the sack of Corinth in 146 B.C.; of another built by Claudius Pulcher in 99 B.C., "so realistically designed that birds came to perch on the painted roof"; and of silver, gold, and ivory decorations used on the scene-walls of the declining Republic. The elder Pliny, writing long after the event, describes the temporary theatre built by Marcus Aemilius Scaurus in 58 B.C. It had "three stories, supported on three hundred and sixty columns . . . the lowest level being of marble, the second of glass, and the uppermost of gilded wood. The columns of the lowest tier were thirty-eight feet high; standing between them were three thousand bronze statues. The theatre had a capacity of eighty thousand." Even after making every allowance for exaggeration, we cannot escape the impression of extravagance run mad.

Three years later, in 55 B.C., Gnaeus Pompeius Magnus, Pompey the Great, used his immense personal prestige to give Rome a permanent stone theatre, an amenity which other Italian cities had enjoyed for centuries. It was built on the reclaimed floodland of the Campus Martius. Though the building itself has disappeared, its design is known from the *Forma Urbis,* a marble plan of the city dating from the second century A.D., and aerial photography reveals the outline of the auditorium (*cavea*) in the pattern of the later streets. Pompey's theatre enjoyed enduring fame. Even after it had ceased to be unique, it was still known simply as "the theatre." In the first century A.D., it was rededicated by the Emperor Claudius; by the third, it had a procurator specially appointed to supervise its upkeep; and at the end of the fourth, when much of the original fabric had collapsed, it suffered wholesale renovation. During its long existence it served as the home of increasingly elaborate spectacles and was still mentioned in the guide books of the Middle Ages.

Pompey conceived his theatre as part of a larger architectural complex, including a senate house, a private house, and gardens universally praised, whose bedding trenches have been uncovered by modern archaeologists. Behind the theatre stood a colonnaded square where the audience could shelter under awnings from the rain. A fraction of this has been uncovered—perhaps the very spot where Caesar met the daggers of his assassins—and may be seen from the pedestrian underpass at one corner of the Largo Argentina, near the ruins of unidentified Republican temples. This propinquity is suggestive. Pompey had chosen a site with long-established religious associations. Even more suggestive is the fact that the theatre embodied a temple to Venus: as shown on the *Forma Urbis,* this stood at the rear of the *cavea,* looking across the audience to the stage. This combination of theatre and temple has been attributed to Pompey's political ingenuity. It is often argued, following a hostile comment in Tertullian, that this was his way of bringing the project to completion despite the puritan opposition; the seats of the theatre, the really objectionable part of the design in austere Roman eyes, were passed off as steps leading to the temple. From what we know of the locations of the earlier, temporary, theatres, it is more likely that Pompey was following prevailing custom, and that the connection between the theatre and organized religion was still a powerful one.

Pompey's model was the Greek Theatre of Mitylene, on the island of Lesbos, which so impressed him on his tour of duty in the East that he formed the project of reproducing it in Rome on a grander scale. Monumental building of this type had become almost obligatory for Roman conquerors, and Pompey was not blind to the political advantages of public works. As the Theatre of Mitylene has vanished without trace, we do not know how strong the influence was. There was, however, one notable departure from Greek practice which had presumably been evident in the temporary theatres also. The Greek theatres, as we have seen, normally utilized the natural slope of the ground and fanned the auditorium up the convenient hillside. Pompey, like most Roman theatre builders, constructed his monument on the flatland, supporting his auditorium on the massive vaults that Roman architects were learning how to employ.

The *cavea* itself was semicircular, divided, as the *Forma Urbis* shows, into thirty-two wedge-shaped sections by lateral aisles and ascending stairs in the customary manner. The Roman theatre, like Roman society, was more class-conscious than the Greek, and different sections of the *cavea* were allotted to the various orders. Horace was later to write disapprovingly of authors and actors who played to the "buyers of roasted beans and chestnuts" at the cost of offending the upper classes and respectable bourgeoisie. He also records a performer who did not care what the rest of the audience did, as long as there was applause from the best seats. We see that the *orchestra,* too, had now been reduced to a semicircle, the logical result of the encroachment made on the original circular form in Hellenistic times. Each wing of the auditorium abutted so closely onto the scene-house that the whole must now be considered not as a collection of separate elements but as one architectural unit.

Cicero, who attended the dedication ceremonies, comments at length on the program but says nothing of the theatre. Among the plays were revivals of old tragedies, so spectacularly mounted that the actors were lost: "For what enjoyment can be had from the sight of six hundred mules in *Clytemnaestra* [by Accius], three thousand bowls in *The Trojan Horse* [by Livius Andronicus], or infantry and cavalry fighting a major engagement in heavy armour?" These were followed by wild-beast hunts, which Cicero despised, with the last day given over to elephants. We would be happy for less acrimony and more description. Other theatres soon followed Pompey's, however, and from their remains and contemporary description we can assemble a composite picture of the stage buildings of the time.

Pompey's device of backing his theatre with a square which served both as *alfresco* lobby and, protected with awnings, as a shelter from rain, was widely known elsewhere. We see the same plan in the larger of the two theatres at Pompeii, a town which, because of its Greek leanings, boasted a permanent place for performances a century and a half before Pompey built his at Rome. The theatre at Ostia, built by Augustus' friend and aide Marcus Agrippa, backs onto a large colonnaded square with a temple in the center, the *piazza delle corporazione,* which did double duty as the city's business center and the theatre's foyer. A similar plan may be seen in Volterra, in Tuscany, where the theatre, one of the finest surviving examples, dates from the late first century A.D.

For the facade, we may examine the remains of the Theatre of Marcellus, near the Roman Forum. This had a complicated history. Julius Caesar, anxious to emulate Pompey, had projected a theatre to be carved, in the Greek manner, out of the Tarpeian Rock, where early Roman criminals were hurled to their deaths. This was never completed. Augustus finished the theatre on a new site nearer the Tiber, where it was linked with the Temple of Apollo. A temporary theatre had perhaps occupied the site earlier, in 179 B.C. Augustus' building was in use for the Secular Games of 17 B.C., while Greek drama played at Pompey's theatre, but the official dedication did not follow until four years later; Augustus named it after his nephew and heir presumptive, Marcus Claudius Marcellus.

The elaborate structural techniques used by Pompey were apparently still novel. At one performance in the Theatre of Marcellus the audience panicked, thinking that the building was about to collapse. Order was only restored when Augustus went down personally to sit in the most dangerous area. Restored by Vespasian after the Great Fire of Rome, the theatre was eventually encrusted with shops, as it continued to be until Mussolini's time; stones were being purloined to repair the nearby bridge in A.D. 375. Augustus' theatre did not last as long as Pompey's. Much had already gone by the Middle Ages, when the building was turned into a castle; more has vanished since, including a vaulted hallway adjoining the outer wall, which still appears in a sixteenth-century print but is no longer visible. Two magnificent tiers of the arched facade remain, however (though still crowned with houses), to show what the theatre must have looked like at its prime. The ingenious system of superimposed arcades looks forward to the complexities of the Colosseum.

The Romans were devising new ways of controlling audiences. The Theatre of Marcellus, as the plan on the *Forma Urbis* shows, used a system of tunnels within the fabric to lead the spectators directly into the center of the *cavea*. The doors through which they entered were known as *vomitoria,* from the way in which they spewed out the crowds. At Ostia, the theatre originally had only two galleries and two side entrances through vaulted corridors. This evidently presented problems, for, in a later reconstruction, a central vaulted entrance was added leading straight under the *cavea* to the *orchestra*. But *vomitoria* remained the common method of channeling off a large crowd, and examples in the theatres and amphitheatres are frequent.

The *scaena* had now grown extremely elaborate; that of the Theatre of Minturnae, south of Rome on the Campanian border, had fourteen rooms. Its facade, as at Pompeii, still had the standard three doors, with another leading in from each wing, though these had now begun to assume a new significance. The central, or "royal" door, as it was now known, was decorated, according to Vitruvius, like that of a palace; the side doors represented guest chambers. Obviously this identification could not have held good for every play. It is a pointer, however, to the increasingly ornate spectacles offered by the Roman theatre. The Emperor Tiberius erected a statue of Augustus over the "royal" door of the Theatre of Marcellus: Augustus had similarly honored Pompey in the theatre that the general had built. Remains at Ostia and elsewhere show that the whole *frons scaenae* was richly decorated with niches and statues. Vitruvius also talks of "three kinds of scene, tragic, comic, and satyric," involving different layouts and decoration. Tragic scenes, he says, are "painted with columns, pediments, statues, and other objects suitable for royalty; comic scenes show private houses with balconies and vistas of windows . . . ; satyric scenes are decorated with trees, caves, mountains, and other rustic objects." Vitruvius does not tell us whether these scenes were painted on removable panels and displayed between permanent uprights in the Hellenistic manner or confined to the *periaktoi* (devices for changing scenery).

The facade of the stage platform was of stone also, with niches for statues and steps going down to *orchestra* level. At Ostia and elsewhere, however, the stage floor was still of wood. This seems to have remained common practice: we can see how it looked from the theatre at Benevento, reconstructed for annual summer performances. At Pompeii the theatre had a stage curtain, rising from a long slot in the stage which may still be seen; it seems also that various smaller curtains *(siparia)* could be used to conceal part of the stage setting until needed. Over the auditorium hung an awning to protect spectators from the sun: Pliny notes this as a Campanian invention, and a Pompeiian painting shows such an awning hanging over the gladiatorial amphitheatre. Lucretius, who gives evidence for the practice in late Republican times, speaks of the "yellow, scarlet, and purple awnings" hanging from poles and rafters over the theatre and washing the stage and *cavea* with color. At Pompeii, the awning of the larger theatre was slung from masts which sprouted from the topmost tiers: we know from references elsewhere that the necessary ropework was done, appropriately, by sailors. Pompey's theatre almost certainly had such an awning from the beginning. We know at least that it possessed one in A.D. 66, when Nero gave a gala performance for the reception of King Tiridates of Armenia. It bore the picture of Nero driving a chariot, surrounded by golden stars. The theatres were magnificent, but Horace, like Cicero, complains of the quality of the programs: he is forced to sit for four and five hours watching parades of infantry and cavalry, captive kings, chariots, carts, wagons, ships; the audience is more interested in giraffes and elephants than in plays. And Horace can still write of the rabble calling out in the middle of a play, "Bring on the bears! Bring on the boxers!" Some things had not changed since Terence's time.

CHAPTER FIVE

⧈

The Roman Actor

The Mask

Any examination of Roman acting must begin with the question of when the actors first wore masks. The evidence is late, uncertain, and contradictory. Diomedes the grammarian and Donatus the literary critic, both writing in the fourth century A.D., ascribe the introduction of the mask variously to Roscius, whose performances were enjoyed by Cicero a century after Terence died, or to Cincius Faliscus and Minucius Prothymus, whose dates are not known. Diomedes asserts that Roscius introduced the mask to disguise his squint. For the squint itself, we have Cicero's corroborative evidence—Roscius, though a powerful actor, was evidently no matinee idol—but Diomedes' story must be suspect as another of those attempts to personalize history that bedevil classical scholarship. Roscius, as Rome's most illustrious actor (Cicero remarks that his name became synonymous with perfection in any profession), might appropriately be credited with devices whose true origins were no longer discernible. In the same way, Aeschylus, the first Athenian playwright whose works were officially preserved, was said to have originated several features of the theatre that we now know to have been in existence before his time.

If the evidence of Diomedes is suspect, that of Donatus is self-contradictory: he asserts elsewhere that Ambivius Turpio, long before Roscius, used masks for Terence's *The Eunuch* and *The Brothers*. Cicero contributes to the confusion by implying that even Roscius could, on occasion, act without a mask. In inquiring, then, whether masks were already in regular use in the time of Plautus and Terence, we must fall back on more general considerations. The fact that Naevius, Plautus' contemporary and, perhaps, collaborator, wrote a play called *Personata* (*The Masked Comedy*) is no evidence one way or the other. More suggestive are the descriptions of characters in the earlier *fabula Atellana* (see p. 94), which hint at the use of masks, and the *phlyakes* paintings, which show conclusively that masked actors were well known in Italy in pre-Plautine times. For some types of performances at least, the mask was already an established convention. Secondly, masks were essential to the Greek plays from the beginning. The Romans adapted the other features of the Greek theatre wholesale: the plots, the familiar range of characters, the shape of the theatre, and even the technical vocabulary in such words as *scaena, proscaenium, choragus,* and *palin* ("encore"). It is difficult to conceive that they would not have taken over, along with the rest, the masks that Greek actors and audiences took for granted. Thirdly, masks would have been invaluable in the "mistaken-identity" plots that are commonplace in Graeco-Roman comedy, and that Plautus develops so effectively in *Amphitruo* and *The Twin Menaechmi.* Here we can only say that masks would have been useful but not essential. Shakespeare could write his *Comedy of Errors* without them and create a maskless Viola, who could, with the audience's indulgence, pass for the living image of Sebastian. The likelihood remains, however, that the availability of masks in the Roman as in the Greek theatre continued to facilitate the identical-twin plot.

One contrary argument often raised in this connection adduces the frequent references to changes of expression in Roman comedy as evidence that the features were uncovered. In Terence's *Phormio,* the slave is encouraging the nervous youth to face his father boldly:

ANTIPHO: Suppose I pretend. Is that good enough?
GETA: You're wasting my time.
ANTIPHO: Look at my face. Hmm! Is that enough now?
GETA: No.
ANTIPHO: What about that?
GETA: You're getting closer.
ANTIPHO: What about that?
GETA: That's about right. Hold on to that one.

It is true that changes of expression are indicated, but this does not necessarily imply that they were seen by the audience. There are any number of similar references in Greek drama, where we know that the actors wore masks from the beginning. Characters are asked why they frown and turn pale and may speak of each other as weeping. Such references are essential in a masked drama, where the only means of indicating a change of facial expression is to talk about it. What cannot be shown must be said. Thus the similar references in Roman comedy are ambiguous and may be taken as evidence for masks just as well as evidence against them. Quintilian, writing at the end of the first century A.D., notes a compromise between the rigidity of the mask and the natural flexibility of facial expression: an old man's mask with one eyebrow raised and the other normal, so that the actor could play with the appropriate profile toward the audience, and his face would seem to change.

The Roman Actor

The Roman actor inherited the Hellenistic acting tradition and was guided by the same principles in the practice of his art. We see the same insistence on the importance of rhythm in movement and delivery. Cicero notes that "if an actor makes a movement that is a little out of time with the music, or extends or curtails the proper length of a verse by a single syllable, he is booed off the stage." He also quotes a favorite saying of Roscius, that "the older he gets, the slower he will make the flute accompaniment, and the lighter the music." This suits well with what we know of the high musical content of the Roman popular comedy (see p. 98), and we may, perhaps, suppose an almost continuous flute accompaniment to the performance, or at least to the major speeches, giving precision and rhythm to the actor's gestures. Acting, song, and dance were still close kin.

Another legacy from Greek times was the close connection between acting and oratory: hardly surprising, since the Roman art of rhetoric was an extension and amplification of Greek practice and inspired by Greek teachers. This gives us valuable information about the stage, for both Cicero, in the first century B.C., and Quintilian, in the first century A.D., base much of their advice to the orator on contemporary theatrical practice. Cicero, defending Roscius' brother-in-law, sees his own appearance in court as a "performance" and affects to find it wanting by comparison with that of the actor, who is also present. "In an orator," he says, "we must demand . . . a tragedian's voice, and the bearing, one might almost say, of the consummate actor." The public speaker, in short, must have the carriage, elegance, stage presence, and technical virtuosity of Roscius, whom Cicero takes as virtually his complete image of the orator, given certain modifications necessary to adapt stage technique to the rostrum. "The speaker's delivery needs to be controlled by posture, gesture, facial expression, and changing intonations of voice; the importance of that item alone is demonstrated by the actor's trivial art on the stage."

While the orator must beware of carrying his mimicry to the lengths necessary for the stage, it is equally important not to go too far to the other extreme. "I dwell on these points because this whole branch of the art has been abandoned by the orators, who are players with real life for their script, and taken over by the actors who only mimic reality." Quintilian, writing for a later age, is more censorious about the need for avoiding theatricality; but he holds up the actor as a useful, if qualified, example, and by telling the orator what to avoid, often gives us useful information about what the actor did.

It has already been suggested that the story of Livius Andronicus' mimed performance shows the importance of gesture to the Roman actor from the earliest times. This is substantiated by a lengthy passage in Plautus' *Miles Gloriosus*, where one character comments on the gestures employed by another. Periplectomenus describes the actions of the slave Palaestrio, who has stepped aside to formulate a plan. He strikes his breast with his fingers "as if to summon forth his heart" (Quintilian is later to outlaw this very gesture as unbecoming for the orator); turns away; lays his left hand on his left thigh; counts on the fingers of his right hand; slaps his right thigh; snaps his fingers (or cracks his knuckles, *digitis concrepuit*); constantly shifts his position; shakes his head as though rejecting an idea; and props his chin in his hands. The whole passage suggests, in fact, the necessity for bodily movement that would be imposed on the actor by the mask.

"Look at that for a graceful pose!" remarks Periplectomenus, "Just like the slaves in the comedies!" This suggests that there were stock attitudes for various types of characters, as familiar to the audience as the masks themselves. Support for this comes from Horace's comment on how to "act the Davus in the comedies, and stand with bowed head like a man much overawed." Davus appears as a slave character in Terence. In *The Art of Poetry*, Horace cautions the writer to use only the modes of diction and expression affirmed by tradition as suitable for each stereotype, and we may reasonably assume traditional gestures and postures as well. Quintilian acknowledges the same principle when he notes how "on the stage, old and young men, soldiers and married women all walk sedately, while slaves, serving-maids, parasites, and prostitutes employ more lively movements." Such basic character movements must have formed the nucleus of the more sustained *lazzi*, whose presence we can detect frequently in Plautine, and occasionally in Terentian comedy; the familiar motif, for example, of the *servus currens*, or running slave, who rushes across the stage with his tunic hitched up around his waist, shouting at the passers-by to clear the way, and so obsessed with his errand that he is deaf to all voices, even that of the man he is supposed to be seeking. Another example is the beating scene, which occurs in virtually every comedy.

Together with postures appropriate to various types of character we may also trace a recognized code of gestures, in the Greek manner, expressive of specific emotions. Some of these involving the deployment of the costume, have already been noted in Chapter Four. The plays suggest others, notably the familiar posture of supplication which is taken over unchanged from Greek practice. A tragic fragment by Accius indicates the gesture, also inherited from the Greek, of tearing the hair in mourning. Seneca writes of "actors in the theatre who imitate the emotions; who portray fear and timidity, depict sorrow, and mimic bashfulness by hanging their heads, lowering their voices, and keeping their eyes fixed on the ground." Such gestures must have been vividly evocative, as Cicero implies when he cautions the orator against overindulgence in their use; he should employ "not the stage gesture which reproduces the words, but one which conveys the general situation and idea, by a hint rather than by mimicry." Quintilian, who urges the orator to cultivate the art that conceals art, implies that on the stage the art was apparent.

The gestures prescribed by Quintilian for the orator, however, suggest how complex the actor's movements must have been. Stress is laid on the carriage of the head, which "drooping suggests humility, and thrown back indicates arrogance; inclined to one side it gives an impression of languor, and when held too rigidly suggests violent temper; but to confine gesture to hand movements alone is regarded as a fault by acting coaches as well as by professors of rhetoric . . . as for the hands, it is scarcely possible to describe the variety of their movements, since they are almost as expressive as words." Quintilian will not let his orator clap his hands or beat his breast, as the actors do, and cautions against raising the hand above eye level or dropping it below breast level. We may surmise that stage gesture was consistently livelier, and at times virtually acrobatic. Even for the orator, Quintilian stipulates the same necessity for abstinence and physical training that we have seen in Greece.

When contrasted with the disarming naturalness of modern oratory, the gestures permitted by Cicero and Quintilian certainly seem theatrical enough. Cicero advises that the arm should be thrown forward "like an elocutionary missile," and the foot stamped for emphasis. Quintilian goes into more detail. The arms should be slightly extended, with the fingers outspread, for running narrative and explicatory passages, and thrown wide for moments of particular emphasis. Successive arguments should be numbered on the fingers (recalling Palaestrio's gesture in *Miles Gloriosus*). The left hand should never be used alone. Both together are more effective. The arms can be raised in adoration, thrown forward in demonstration, or averted, to express horrified rejection. Even the deployment of the fingers is considered in considerable detail. Both actor and orator were evidently intended to perform as human semaphores, telegraphing their emotions to the audience through the activity of the entire body. It has been claimed that a number of these evocative gestures, which are in fact only an artistic heightening of the pantomime which accompanies everyday Italian conversation, could still be traced among the Neapolitans of the nineteenth century; they certainly found their way, with the rediscovery of Quintilian in the Renaissance, into the oratorical practice of Western Europe, and directly influenced the style of Elizabethan acting. On one point Cicero and Quintilian disagree. The former argues that the appropriate gesture should follow the words rather than accompanying them (as, by implication, on the stage); the latter, that words and movement should be simultaneous.

This emphasis on movement does not mean that the voice was neglected. Cicero can still speak of acting in the Aristotelian manner, as among those arts "in which nothing is expected but the gratification of the ear," and remarks on the rigorous exercises undergone by the Greek tragedians of his time. They "practice declamation in a sitting position for years, and every day, before they go onstage, lie down and gradually force their voices up the scale. Later, after playing their parts, they seat themselves and bring their voices down again from the highest treble to the lowest bass." This description stresses not only the rigor but the artificiality of the performance; there was still a "tragic voice" that was the product of conscious art. It is appropriate to recall here that even the recitation of Vergil was held to require special and elaborate training. Tragic declamation at Rome was still slow and stately. Quintilian distinguishes between the rapid delivery of Roscius, primarily a comic performer, and the more ponderous style of Aesopus the tragedian. It is clear that comedy at least admitted a high degree of vocal impersonation. Cicero comments on the quavering voice of Roscius in old man parts, while Quintilian notes that the delivery of comic actors, while still betraying art, was not too remote from the speech patterns of everyday life. It is clear, too, that Plato's strictures on excessive vocal imitation could still apply; actors are censured for adopting the voices of characters that they quote.

We may see the Roman actors, then, as substantially following the Hellenistic tradition. While accepting a system of conventional gestures and delivery, they modified it with their own particular talents, and, at least in the case of the stars, allowed their idiosyncrasies to obtrude. Quintilian writes how Demetrius "showed his unique talents in the movement of his hands, his power to charm his audience with extended and mellifluous imitations, the skill with which he would seem to make the wind puff out his costume as he walked, and the occasional expressive move-

ments of the right side which he introduced with effect." Strato-
cles, on the other hand, was known for "his nimbleness and rapid-
ity of movement, his laugh (which he deliberately used to
provoke an answering laugh from the audience, though it was not
always in character), and his trick of sinking his neck into his
shoulders." Such were the tricks, apparently, that the audience
came to see. Horace had already remarked that the spectators
were more impressed by a fine costume than by anything the actor said.

We are still talking, clearly, of "technical" actors, and an art
that was founded on externals. Those who had thoroughly mastered these externals, however, could sometimes identify themselves powerfully with the emotions they were portraying. Cicero
writes of the actor's eyes blazing behind the mask, and Quintilian
of performers weeping as they left the stage after some particularly emotional scene. Plutarch adds a story which must represent
the apogee of "Method" acting: Aesopus, while playing Atreus
plotting revenge against his brother, lashed out with his scepter at
a servant who was running across the stage and struck him dead.

From Cicero we also glean some familiar hints of what star
temperament could mean, and of the master-disciple relationship
which still persisted in the training of actors. We hear of small
part players required to moderate their voices so as not to detract
from the principal, and of actors excusing their off-days on the
grounds that they were under the weather, or not in the mood.
We see a Roscius who was in demand as a teacher hardly less than
as a performer, who developed the mediocre talents of Eros into
star quality, but who was testy with his pupils and complained
that he had never found one worthy of him. We learn too that, in
spite of the almost hysterical adulation lavished on the idols of the
moment, the condition of the average actor had hardly improved
from the time of Plautus to the Empire. Antiphon, whose performance was witnessed by Cicero in 54, was originally a slave:
Cicero notes that he was liberated just before coming onstage.
Panurgus, another slave-actor, was trained by Roscius, who
owned him jointly with Fannius Chaeraea. When this promising

investment died, Fannius sued Roscius for negligence. Cicero, defending his idol, pays ample tribute to Roscius' ability—Fannius' share in the deceased, he says, was worth no more than 4,000 sesterces, while Roscius' contribution was worth one hundred thousand—but demonstrates in doing so that the actor's status was little better than that of the slave girl educated in music to fetch a higher price. For all his admiration of Roscius, Cicero can still refer to his art as trivial and turn a personal compliment into a slight on the profession: "for just as Roscius is such an artist that he alone seems worthy of being seen on the stage, so is he such a man that he alone seems worthy of never appearing on it." And Seneca, writing in the next century in the reign of a notable theatrical amateur sneers at the professional actor who is an emperor onstage and a slave off, with five measures of grain and five denarii for his wages.

Dramatic Forms: Comedy and Tragedy

The oratorical writers take their illustrations principally from comedy, not only because it comes closest to the pattern of everyday speech, but because it is most easily accessible to them and their readers. By the end of the Republic, tragedy retained little hold on the public affection. Roscius, though he occasionally appeared in tragedy, was primarily a comic actor. One of his favorite parts was the pimp Ballio in Plautus' *Pseudolus*. Greek tragedies of the past were still revived but the performances were now swamped with spectacle, or marred by bursts of irreverence. Horace tells the story of a revival of the ghost play *Iliona*, by Pacuvius. The actor Fufius, playing Iliona, came on drunk and fell so soundly asleep that he failed to hear the summons of the ghost. As one man, the whole audience bellowed the line.

Under the Empire, tragedy became more and more the amusement of a coterie audience. Most of the original tragedies of this period have been lost: Ovid's *Medea*, greatly admired in its time, survives, if at all, only in a plot outline preserved by the elder Seneca, a professor of rhetoric. The only remaining examples of imperial tragedy are the works of Seneca the Younger, mostly modeled on known Greek originals and bearing the stamp of the rhetorical schools, where the average Roman youth passed most of his education. Whether these plays were written for performance on the public stage is a vexed and probably insoluble question. Some of them call for effects which even Roman extravagance and ingenuity would find it hard to reproduce: all of them seem oblivious to certain basic requirements of an acting script. It is often hard to see when the entrances are supposed to occur, who is talking to whom, and who is on stage at any given time. Senecan tragedy has enjoyed a number of modern revivals, but these, of course, tell us nothing of the author's original intentions. It is safe to assume that these plays were intended not for the stage but for reading performances and private recitals, probably in the schools of rhetoric of which Seneca's father had been a distinguished light. Consequently, though they reproduce a number of the stylistic and structural devices of Greek tragedy, they tell us nothing about the nature of tragic acting under the Empire.

We learn a little more from the biographies of Nero, whom Seneca served as tutor, ghost-writer, and advisor. The Emperor was a keen amateur performer. He had a private theatre in his palace, where he played tragedies in which the masks were modeled after members of his intimate circle. It has recently been suggested that the whole story of Nero's murder of his mother derives from a garbled account of such a performance of the Orestes story, in which Nero played the matricidal hero and the actor playing Clytemnestra was masked as Agrippina. Nor were Nero's talents confined to private theatricals. He competed as actor and singer, with predictable success, in festivals both in Italy and abroad. We have an account of his voice-training exercises, at least as rigorous as those of the Greeks, including lying flat with heavy weights on his chest to improve breath control. We have a brief, vivid impression of the pompous and inflated nature of Roman tragedy in the story of a rustic spectator who was so alarmed to see the masked and padded emperor swaggering onto the stage that he ran from the theatre in panic.

Tragedy had become a caricature of itself. This impression is reinforced by the satirist Lucian, who wrote a century after Nero but clearly described a similar type of performance. In his dialogue *On the Dance*, he professes to find the outward semblance of tragedy ridiculous. The actor is padded to increase his bulk (such padding is also described by Pollux): he is wearing a horrific mask, with gaping mouth and *onkos*, or high-piled hair; on his feet are stilt-like shoes, to give him additional stature; and he declaims his part in a sing-song, which Lucian finds ridiculous in a hero such as Heracles. This grotesque kind of performance was, unfortunately, to color popular ideas of classical tragedy long afterward.

CHAPTER SIX

▣

The Entertainment
of the Later
Roman World

The Theatres: Modifications and Rebuilding

Theatres proliferated throughout the Roman Empire. Every city of importance had its own. In the areas where Greek influence had been predominant, the Romans modified existing structures to their own taste. In Athens, the Theatre of Dionysos owes its present form largely to the Emperor Nero. During his reign, the *orchestra* was repaved with stone slabs in the familiar diamond pattern, and a new stage was built, thrusting even further forward into the space originally occupied by the chorus. Minor modifications took place in the auditorium for Hadrian's visit in 126 B.C., including the erection of new seats of honor: as at Priene earlier, the seats on the rim of the *orchestra* were found no longer to command a good view. At some subsequent date the front of the stage was adorned with sculptural reliefs, some of which are still in place today: showing episodes from the Dionysos story, they were taken, perhaps, from an earlier altar. The Theatre of Dionysos had by this time become a multipurpose building. It held, at various times, gladiatorial combats and puppet shows; and an elaborate drainage system was introduced, together with the waterproofing of the stage front and surrounding parapet, to allow the *orchestra* to be flooded for aquatic spectacles.

Similar rebuilding took place at Corinth, which retained its importance as a center for international trade. Here the slope of the Greek auditorium was made steeper, covering the original seats with an earth fill, the *orchestra* and the area surrounding the scene-house were repaved, and the *skene* itself was transformed into the customary elaborate Roman structure. As in Athens, provision was made to adapt what remained of the *orchestra* to other purposes. In the early third century A.D., it was used for gladiatorial fights, with the lower tiers of seats removed for the greater safety of the spectators. Here too it was possible for the *orchestra* to be flooded. The earlier Greek construction had already provided one peripheral drain, covered during performance with wooden panels. Another was added during the later Roman period, together with a surrounding parapet. Water was channeled into the *orchestra* from a large reservoir to the east of the stage.

Of the purely Roman constructions in other parts of the Empire, several are still in regular use. In France, the theatres of Arles and Orange house annual summer festivals. Arles (the Roman Arelate) was originally founded as a military colony and may already have possessed a theatre in Julius Caesar's time, though substantial rebuilding was carried out under the later emperors. At Orange the theatre stands beside the circus, a significant juxtaposition at a time when the forms of entertainment were merging to the point where they were sometimes barely distinguishable. At Arles the *scaenae frons* conceals a row of dressing rooms, while at Orange these are concentrated within the towering wings that flank the stage. In other respects the theatres are virtually identical and share the characteristics already described in connection with the theatres of Rome and Italy. These features, indeed, remain constant throughout the Empire. We note the increasing elaboration of the *scaena,* studded with busts and statues of the divinities and the Imperial Family, and the provision of a magnificent *regia* (royal entrance) for the principal actor. Particularly in Africa, the Roman architects sought to break up the plane surface of the *scaena* with columns, thus producing an elusive pattern of light and shadow. Palladio recaptured these qualities in the *teatro olimpico* at Vicenza, where he reconstructed a Roman theatre for Renaissance audiences. We note, too, the gradual enclosure of the audience and the performance from the outside world. In Greece, the theatres had generally evolved naturally out of their physical environment, blending with and utilizing the contours of the land. The Roman theatres, with their high *scaenae* and enclosing walls, placed the spectator from the beginning in a setting that was entirely the product of art. Sir Mortimer Wheeler, in his study of Roman architecture, has emphasized the care devoted to the interiors of buildings, as contrasted with the comparative lack of attention given to the exteriors. If we may revert to the concept of the theatre as an architectural metaphor for the function of drama in society (see p. 16), we may see in the Roman structures the clearest possible statement of the divorcement of art from actuality; of the creation of a purely artificial environment; and of the new function of the drama as spectacle, titillation, and appeasement.

We may see the concept of the enclosed performance particularly in the *odeum* (Greek *odeion*), or recital hall. Such buildings were constructed, often side by side with the larger theatres, with more intimate performances in mind. The smaller theatre at Pompeii is technically such an *odeum:* though it follows the basic pattern of its larger neighbor, it was originally roofed. Another example lies near the theatre at Corinth, to which it was originally linked by colonnades. Similar complexes existed in many Roman cities. The best surviving *odeum,* and certainly the most famous, is that built by and named after Herodes Atticus in Athens. Herodes, a distinguished philosopher and patron of the arts, spread his benefactions throughout Greece but was particularly concerned with the adornment of Athens. His concert hall was begun in A.D. 161 and had the customary features of the Roman theatre: a semicircular *orchestra* entered through *parodoi* under the tiered seating, a raised stage, and a high *scaena*. (An opera singer required to appear in the topmost arch during a recent Athens Festival suffered a severe attack of vertigo.) According to one ancient source, the *odeum* was covered with a roof of cedar wood and precious metals, but it is hard to see how this could have extended over the entire *cavea* (auditorium). Perhaps only the stage had such a canopy, with a separate roof for the auditorium.

The Greek and Roman theatres of Athens thus sat side by side, on the same slope of the Acropolis and linked by a portico erected by King Eumenes II of Pergamum (197–159 B.C.) to provide shelter for the audiences at the Theatre of Dionysos, and subsequently extended to reach Herodes' new *odeum*. Although the Roman theatre comes nowhere near the Greek size (never more than 6,000 spectators, even in antiquity, as opposed to the 17,000 of the Theatre of Dionysos), it provides a venue, more accessible than Epidauros, for the presentation of the ancient plays in an approximation to their original surroundings, and when floodlit for the annual Athens Festival offers a spectacle that would have impressed even its Roman builders.

The Mime

The Roman theatres, as we have seen, held other things besides plays. One of the most popular forms of entertainment was the mime, whose origins reach back to remote antiquity and several of whose affiliations we have already noted in the course of this study. "Mime" in the classical sense (Greek *mimos*, Latin *mimus*) refers not to a silent performer but to one who offered a melange of song, dance and the spoken word akin to the music hall and vaudeville of our own century. Like these later manifestations, the mime performances varied in their dramatic content. The earliest Greek evidence suggests that the mimes may originally have been, like the drama proper, connected with Dionysiac ritual, perhaps presenting scenes from the associated mythology. Certainly an element of myth-burlesque, similar to that of satyr play, seems to have been present from early times. We may also distinguish, from surviving mask replicas and other pictorial evidence, recurring characters such as the fool, the doctor, and the old hag. The "learned man," of course, is one of the most familiar figures of popular comedy and in the classical world most commonly appears as the doctor.

We know that the mime performance embraced all kind of entertainment. At one end of the scale, it was virtually indistinguishable from the literary drama, and at the other involved tumbling, juggling, conjuring, and puppetry. It is as well to remember, however, that in the light of what was said in Chapter Two concerning the acrobatic nature of Greek acting, that the gulf between the mime and the "legitimate" actor was not so wide as it may appear to us. Though it must be admitted that some Greek actors thought such a gulf to exist, and clearly attributed to the mimes an inferior status. We have an amusing story of professional snobbery in Plutarch's account of the tragic actor Callippides, who attempted to thrust himself on the attention of King Agesilaos of Sparta. "Oh yes," retorted Agesilaos crushingly, "you are Callippides the mime." The mime differed from other performances in one conspicuous way: even in the Greek period actresses were allowed and became a well-applauded feature of the Roman troupes.

In discussing a form so generalized as the mime, so rudimentary in its appeal, and so diverse in its manifestations, it is obviously impossible to be precise about time and place, or to distinguish Greek from Italian elements. Performances of this type must have contributed to the development of Old Comedy and provided many of the familiar *lazzi* that Aristophanes builds into his plays. The affiliations with the *phlyakes* and Atellan farces, and the *satura*, which Livy describes as the forerunner of Roman drama, are equally clear. The mime first appears as a distinct literary genre in the work of Epicharmus, a Sicilian writer of the late fifth century B.C. Surviving titles suggest that the playlets were drawn variously from the Homeric cycle, mythology—which they burlesqued—or observations of everyday life. It is the latter class that tends to predominate. Herodas, writing in the first half of the third century B.C., composed dramatic vignettes drawn from his own society. These can be and have been performed; whether the author so intended is dubious. He may simply have transposed the popular form into a purely literary mode, as other writers, notably the Sicilian poet Theocritus, also did. "Mime" means literally "imitation," and was commonly seen as an imitation of everyday life; its natural fondness for vivid material gave it an enduring reputation for indency.

It was in Rome that the mime won greatest recognition. The spectators who walked out of Terence's comedies were probably attracted by some sort of mime show. Although several of its exponents grew rich, an art which had the double disadvantage, in aristocratic eyes, of being both popular and indecent, carried a certain stigma. Its place on the more serious stage was always secondary. Mime players offered after-pieces or interludes in the dramatic festivals: the relationship between mime and the Roman literary drama, in fact, seems to have been broadly similar to that between *kyogen* and Nō in the Japanese tradition, the former providing comic scenes of low life, originally unscripted, as a relief from the more cerebral entertainment of the latter. From time to time the mimes found illustrious sponsors. Appearing on the Roman stage as early as the third century B.C., the mimes were later encouraged by the dictator Sulla, who had a penchant for the theatre, and after him by Julius Caesar. It was, at this point, still no shame to write for them. Decimus Laberius, an *eques*, "knight" (that is, a member of the monied bourgeoisie) of Caesar's time, was one of several who cultivated the mime and attempted, through their compositions, to give it some sort of literary esteem. Acting for the mimes was a different story. Laberius was forced by Caesar to give a "command performance" in one of his own playlets, and we still possess the speech in which he records his own humiliation.

It is clear, from the surviving fragments of Laberius, that the topicality of the mime could still extend to contemporary politics: it was Laberius' license, indeed, in satirizing the dictatorship of Caesar that seems to have provoked his social disgrace. The titles suggest that some of his themes were related to those of Graeco-Roman comedy. *Colax* (*The Parasite*) invokes the familiar New Comic stereotype. *Hecyra* (*Mother-in-Law*) is also the title of a play by Terence. *Phasma* (*The Ghost*) suggests affinities with Plautus' *Mostellaria,* and with Menander. Other titles, *Augur* (*The Augur*), *Fullo* (*The Fuller*), and *Nuptiae* (*The Wedding*), clearly refer to scenes of everyday life. We may assume that the mode of performance, also, could lean more or less heavily on that of the legitimate drama, and that there were still times when the two forms resembled each other. Publius Syrus, the chief rival of Laberius, was, more appropriately in Roman eyes, a freed slave. Although he was chiefly famous for his improvisations, a collection of his witty sayings survived into imperial times as a Roman equivalent of *Joe Miller's Jest Book.*

Of the mime actresses of the late Republic we know two famous names, Arbuscula and Cytheris. The former, mentioned by both Cicero and Horace, was something of a snob, announcing that, as long as the knights applauded, she did not care what the rest of the audience did. Cytheris was taken by Mark Antony as his mistress; Cicero was once shocked to meet her at a dinner party. But though a few ladies of the Empire flouted convention by appearing on the stage, the *mima* was in general regarded as no better than a prostitute. Under a law drafted by Julius Caesar, no son of an actor or actress could be elected as town councilor. The marriage laws devised by Augustus forbade any senator to take a wife from the theatrical profession. Though some of the *mimae* attained eminence—the most famous being Theodora, who began as an actress and ended as Empress of the Eastern Empire—they were compelled to fight popular prejudice at every turn.

Under the Empire, the mimes had the same popularity, and the same inferior social status. Juvenal, in his Eighth Satire, ridicules the infamy of patricians under Nero, who, to flatter their Emperor's well-known predilection for the theatre, performed as actors on the public stage. With them he classes Damasippus and Lentulus, impoverished gentlemen turned mime out of financial necessity. Damasippus played "the squeaking Ghost of Catulus" and Lentulus the part of Laureolus in a play by the same author. This man—his full name was Quintus Lutatius Catulus—flourished during the early Empire, and enjoyed the friendship of the Imperial Family. Several macabre references to his play *Laureolus* indicate that it concerned a criminal condemned to death by crucifixion. Juvenal, describing Lentulus' performance, remarks that it was worthy of a real cross. Martial, commenting on a later revival staged in the Colosseum, shows that this possibility had not escaped the authorities. The mime was reenacted in the amphitheatre with total realism, and Laureolus, "hanging on a cross that was all too real" (*non falsa pendens in cruce*), was played by a condemned criminal who, at the finale, was torn apart by a bear. "What once had been a fiction," says Martial, "became a punishment." Other examples of the combining of dramatic form with the Roman fondness for human slaughter will be considered below.

The infinite variety of the mime performance is perhaps most vividly suggested by a fictional source, *Satyricon* by Petronius, written in the reign of Nero and describing the *nouveaux-riches* of his society. In the famous account of Trimalchio's feast, we see the entertainment offered by a millionaire to his guests. Although the performers are members of the household, their arts suggest those of the public stage. The guests are offered a boy dancer, who imitates various aspects of the god Dionysos, and a mock hunt which ushers in one course of the dinner. Later come rope dancers and a "great brute of a fellow," who holds up a ladder while a boy dances, to sung accompaniment, on the top rung. The same boy then dives through flaming hoops and picks up an amphora in his teeth. Lip service is paid to culture with recitations from Homer (in Greek) and Vergil, though the latter is interspersed with verses from the Atellan farces. In addition, there is a constant succession of mechanical marvels. We may imagine such performances being given in the banquet hall of Nero's Golden House or the private theatre in Domitian's villa at Albano. Trimalchio professes to dislike performing animals, but they were evidently popular with the general public. In the reign of Vespasian, a mime was given in the Theatre of Marcellus with a dog in the leading part. Pliny opens the eighth book of his *Natural History* with a long account of the accomplishments of performing elephants, who could dance, toss weapons in the air, engage in gladiatorial combats, and walk the tightrope. He notes the pathetic story of one beast who was slow learning his part and, after several beatings, was observed in the middle of the night quietly rehearsing by himself. In the late third century, we hear of a mammoth spectacle including rope dancers, bears who acted a play, and flute players, the whole ending with the mock conflagration of the theatre.

Some of the imperial mime actors are known to us by name. Seneca mentions an *archimimus* (leader of a mime troupe) called Doctus; this may be a stage name with reference to the role of the learned man that the actor commonly played. An inscription of A.D. 169 refers to an *archimimus* with the grandiloquent name of Lucius Aelius Pontinus Eutyches, who headed a company of sixty. In the troubled history of early Christianity, the mimes earned more notoriety through their parodies of the rites of the new religion. This kind of topicality, at least, was palatable to the authorities. Some mimes came to mock and remained to pray. Philemon, a favorite performer of the city of Antinoe, was converted during the persecutions of the reign of Diocletian, and for his martyrdom became a saint of the Catholic Church. Genesius suffered the same fate and won the same glory in A.D. 303. But the spirit of the mime, on the whole, was unaffected by religious changes. It has been powerfully argued that those uninhibited performers of the Roman world survived the decline of the pagan theatre to become the troubadours and *jongleurs* of the Middle Ages. An epitaph for the mime Vitalis, found in a ninth-century manuscript (the actual poem, like its subject, is undatable), is a tribute to the carefree talents of the performer, touched with Christian morbidity. We are told of Vitalis' skill in word and gesture and his versatility in presenting a whole succession of different characters: his audiences thought him to be "many men, not one." He is particularly praised for his mimicry of women, whom he can imitate even to the blush. When Vitalis died, the poem concludes, there died with him the thousands of characters he had created.

Pantomime and Dance

In the mime, we have been considering a type of performance which, though it touched the history of the regular drama at various points, for the most part went its own way. With the pantomimes, we come closer to the familiar themes of tragedy. Once again, the meaning of the word has changed. The pantomime of antiquity implied a ballet performance, with one or more dancers, based on some episode from epic or myth. Although this art form reached its full development under the Roman Empire, it was already well known to the Greeks, as a passage from Xenophon shows. The author, a pupil of Socrates and a historian of the Athenian decline, is describing a banquet given in his own house. One of the guests is a puppeteer, described only as "the man from Syracuse"; a traveling mime, perhaps, from the country which bred Epicharmus. At the close of the feast, dancers appear, apparently members of the Syracusan's troupe. A chair is set in the banquet hall and two performers enact the marriage of Dionysos and Ariadne. First comes a solo for Ariadne, "dressed as a bride," who seats herself in the chair and then mimes her ecstasy as she hears the Bacchic music offstage. Dionysos enters dancing, sits on her lap, throws his arms around her, and kisses her. (At this point, the banqueters cry "encore.") The god and his bride then rise and dance together; there is more amorous byplay and, apparently, some spoken dialogue. At the close of what, in spite of Xenophon's decorous account, seems to have been a highly erotic performance, the pair depart as for the bridal chamber, and the guests, inspired to emulation, hurry home to their wives.

The Telestes whose name is mentioned in connection with Aeschylus may have been a performer of this type. As previously noted, it is not clear whether he was a contemporary and collaborator of the poet or a later artist reinterpreting the themes of Aeschylean tragedy in dance form. The Xenophon of Smyrna hailed in a late Greek epigram may be a product of the same tradition. He is praised for his performance as Cadmus, the "messenger from the wood," and Agave in what seems to be a clear reference to Euripides' *The Bacchae*. As an actor, he could not have played all these parts in the same performance, and as the emphasis of the poem is on dancing throughout, it is likely that we are dealing here with a balletic interpretation of the tragedy in which one man, by a change of masks, took several parts. Given the extent to which the legitimate actor relied on dance, performances of this type appear as natural byproducts of the tragic tradition. In the Roman theatre, we have an early precedent in the stories of Livius Andronicus, compelled to employ pantomime through the loss of his voice.

Some late Roman sources claim that the art did not begin until the reign of Augustus. This is clearly untrue, though Lucian, whose account of the dance we shall examine shortly, claims the word "pantomime" as a Roman coinage. Certainly, however, the beginning of the Roman Empire saw the development of the art into its perfected form. Pylades and Bathyllus were well-known dancers under Augustus. There were at least two artists called Paris, which seems to have been a popular stage name, one in the reign of Nero, the other in that of Domitian; both became friends of court. The themes were taken variously from mythic, epic, and tragic sources. *Leda and the Swan* was a particular favorite, doubtless because of its erotic possibilities. Some subjects were taken from Vergil; we hear also of *The Trojan Women* and *Phaedra,* and ballets based on the Hercules and Oedipus stories.

Our most detailed account of the imperial pantomime comes from *The Dance,* by the second-century satirist Lucian. Written in dialogue form, it offers a tribute to the dancer's art as lavish as its denunciation of tragedy (see p. 134) is scathing. Dance, says Lucian, is hallowed by antiquity; it is the terrestrial counterpart of the movement of the spheres, and thus reflects the divine order of things. It figures in the earliest myths of creation and is constantly invoked throughout history to reflect the deeds and preoccupations of mankind. To support his point, Lucian embarks on a catalogue, which is, in effect, a summary of the mythic history of the world, beginning with the creation and embracing the stories of individual cities. His purpose here is two-fold: to give mythic sanction to the art of dance and to provide a sourcebook which will aid both the dancers and librettists and their audiences. Analogies are drawn between the performer and the myths he represents: the dancer is compared, for example, to Proteus, the sea god who could assume any shape at will.

Lucian also gives us a practical exposition of the art as he knew it. The favored form was now the solo performance, in which a single dancer wore a succession of masks: Lucian adds the detail that the pantomime masks had closed mouths, in contrast to their gaping tragic counterparts. We are given the comment of an anonymous barbarian, who, watching a dancer prepare for a performance with five masks, remarked, "I did not realize, my dear sir, that you had only one body, but many souls." The dancer's versatility is constantly impressive.

In general, the dance undertakes to present and enact characters and emotions, introducing the lover one moment, the man enraged the next, now the madman, now the man struck with grief . . . in one and the same day, we are shown first the frenzied Athamas, then the terrified Ino; after a while, the same person becomes Atreus, and the next minute Thyestes; then Aegisthus, or Aerope; yet they are all the same man.

The dancer is accompanied by flute and pipes, taking the beat from the tapping of a wooden or iron-soled shoe. Cymbals may be used and the narrative may be provided by a solo reciter or a small chorus. Such an arrangement is suggested by certain Pompeian wall paintings. For the most part, however, the dancer is required to present the character by his skill in movement and gesture. The audience must be able to "understand the mute, and hear the dancer though he does not talk." Lucian suggests that the dancer might occasionally be confused between different items in his vast repertoire, quoting the case of one pantomime who, presenting the birth of Zeus with Cronus eating his children, was misled by the similarity of incidents and went on with the story of Thyestes. It goes without saying that the dancer must have great physical stamina. Lucian quotes several stories of performers who lacked the requisite stature for their roles. When a small man appeared to dance Hector, the audience shouted "We can see Astyanax; where's Hector?"

According to Lucian, the dancer might become totally, and terrifyingly, involved in his performance. He quotes the story of one man portraying the madness of Ajax who went berserk, tore the clothes off his accompanist, seized the iron-soled shoe, and cracked the head of his partner, who was playing Odysseus. Macrobius, some three centuries later, tells a similar story of a dancer portraying the madness of Heracles. Annoyed by the jeers of the audience, he turned on them and shot his arrows into their midst.

The pantomimes fluctuated in official esteem. Tiberius suppressed private shows, but Caligula reintroduced them: Domitian forbade public performances but allowed the dancers to perform in private. Pantomimic contests seem to have figured in some of the public games: records suggest that they were included in the *ludi* at Naples. Certainly the pantomimes endured in popularity. Memories of these performances, together with the attested fondness of playwrights for giving public readings of their works, undoubtedly contributed to one curious misconception of the classical drama that was widespread in the Middle Ages: that the plays were not performed in the ordinary sense but declaimed by the poet or a reader from a central podium, while mute performers mimed the appropriate action.

The Amphitheatre: Gladiatorial Combats and Beast Hunts

Among the other forms of entertainment in the Roman Empire, the circuses, being purely athletic in nature, do not fall within the compass of this book. We may legitimately include the amphitheatres, however, as the gladiatorial combats and beast shows came in time to acquire a distinctly dramatic coloration and merge, as we have already seen in the case of *Laureolus*, with other types of performance. Gladiatorial combat was introduced from Etruria (see p. 95) and first appears in Roman society in connection with funeral rites. In its original form, it undoubtedly represents a survival of the primitive belief that the prominent dead could be assured attendance in the after-life by the ritual slaughter of a number of their inferiors. The first recorded combat in Rome occurred in 264 B.C., when three pairs of gladiators fought at the funeral games given for Marcus Brutus by his sons. Ninety years later, at the funeral of Titus Flaminius, there were thirty-seven pairs. The new spectator sport caught on rapidly: a hundred pairs of gladiators were offered by Julius Caesar when, as *aedile* (magistrate), he sponsored the public games. There was no longer any question of honoring the dead. The gladiatorial games had become a show in their own right and demanded special places where they could be held.

The beast hunts (*venationes*) appealed to a similar mentality and enjoyed the same rapid rise in public esteem. The first Roman *venatio* was offered by Marcus Fulvius Nobilior after his conquest of Aetolia in 186 B.C., with lions and panthers hunted to death for the amusement of the crowd. In 169 B.C., at games given jointly by Publius Cornelius Scipio Nasica and Publius Lentulus, sixty-three beasts were killed, including panthers, bears, and elephants. There was another show in 146 B.C. to celebrate the final defeat of Carthage. In 58 B.C., Marcus Aemilius Scaurus exhibited 150 beasts of all kinds, including a hippopotamus and five crocodiles in a specially constructed basin. In 55 B.C., at the inauguration of

Pompey's theatre (the performance witnessed by Cicero, see p. 118) the audience saw a rhinoceros, a lynx from Gaul, and a rare monkey from Africa. There was a growing demand for the more exotic animals; in 46 B.C., at Caesar's triumph, Romans saw a giraffe for the first time.

The earlier gladiatorial games, as we learn from Vitruvius, were held in the Forum, and the *venationes* in the Forum or circuses. All exits were barred off, and the people watched from the roofs or balconies of adjoining houses. The spectacle must have been similar to the bull-running in the streets of Pamplona in our own time. When special buildings were called for, the architects applied the principles already familiar from theatre construction: the customary form of the amphitheatre (and hence its name) is of two theatres brought face to face, creating a central oval (the *arena,* so called from the sand that covered it and could be raked over to disguise the traces of bloodshed) completely surrounded

Nîmes, Roman amphitheatre, showing seating and *vomitoria*.

by tiers of seats. We may assume wooden prototypes for the stone amphitheatres, as for the theatres themselves; even some of the later examples seem to preserve the features of wooden construction. The oldest permanent amphitheatre of which we have any knowledge was built at Pompeii about 80 B.C., by Gaius Quinctus Volgus and Marcus Porcius, the same magistrates who were responsible for the construction of the smaller theatre. Pressure of space was evidently the cause of a lack of symmetry in the building. There are other notable differences between this amphitheatre and later examples. The principal stairways, which elsewhere are carried inside the fabric, are here placed less conveniently against the exterior walls; and there is no sign of the usual substructure of beast cages and underground passages. This suggests either a necessary economy in the construction, or, more probably, the fact that the beast shows, at least in the south, did not yet have the wide popularity they were later to acquire, so that it was unnecessary to make special provision for them. As already noted (see p. 121) the audience was protected from the sun by awnings slung from masts projecting from the upper walls. When originally built, the amphitheatre had a capacity far greater than the population of Pompeii and was evidently designed to attract spectators from the surrounding area.

Other amphitheatres soon followed: Rome had its first in 46 B.C., a temporary structure ascribed to Caesar's lieutenant Curio. The first stone building was erected in 29 B.C. by Statilius Taurus; by this time, amphitheatres were being constructed throughout the Roman world. The gladiators who fought in them were, for the most part, selected slaves, trained in a special school under a master of arms (*lanista*). At Pompeii, the colonnaded square behind the large theatre was taken over, in Nero's time, for such a school. The gladiators lived in cell-like rooms on two storys: the main gateway is suspiciously narrow, to prevent escapes. Training was rigorous. Archaeologists have uncovered a punishment room, fitted with stocks and manacles. The Ludus Magnus, the largest gladiatorial school in Rome itself, has been excavated more recently and confirms the fact that the slave chosen for such purposes could expect little but hardship. He had at least the consolation of knowing that his performance in the arena might win him the adulation of the masses—a number of the Pompeiian inscriptions so testify—and, if he were lucky, his freedom: the gladiator with a run of victories might be awarded the wooden sword (*rudis*) and his liberty. It was not unknown, however, for free citizens in need of money to hire themselves out to fight in the arena. There were also distinguished amateurs. The Emperor Commodus loved to display himself as a gladiator and, not surprisingly, won all his bouts.

The great disadvantage of the gladiatorial bouts as public entertainment was that the simple act of slaughter was repetitious, monotonous, and eventually cloying. The sponsors attempted to alleviate this by varying the methods of combat. Gladiators would fight in full armor or naked, from a chariot, or with net and trident. We may judge from the comments of Seneca, however, that the audience was more interested in bloodshed than skill. He writes of how the crowd welcomed the midday combats, when condemned criminals were forced to fight to the death in the intervals between the formal bouts. The greater the skill of the combatants, the slower the death. Similarly with the *venationes:* we see a growing desperation on the part of the sponsors in their desire to find more and more exotic beasts to slaughter. It is at this point that the "blood sports" may be placed in a dramatic frame of reference. To provide spectacle and variety, the sponsors began to give the combats scripts and set the beast hunts in elaborate settings designed to recall a favorite myth. We may compare, perhaps, the similar history of all-in wrestling in our own time, where many combatants now assume fantastic costumes and acquire distinct dramatic personalities.

The lengths to which such spectacles could go are shown by stories of the early Empire. Seneca is clearly writing of the amphitheatre when he classes with the arts of amusement "the stage machinists who invent scaffolding that rises under its own power, and floors that ascend noiselessly into the air, and a diversity of other surprises, such as objects that fit together and split apart again, or separate units assembling themselves automatically, or lofty structures gradually collapsing." Nero flooded his amphitheatre with sea water, filling it with fish and "sea monsters." A naval battle then took place between men representing the Persians and Athenians. Following this, the water was drawn off, the arena dried out, and contests staged between land forces.

Such mimic sea fights were favorite attractions. Augustus, who also mentions in his account of his reign that he had given twenty-six *venationes*, offered such a spectacle in a specially constructed basin on the right bank of the Tiber. We have a long and circumstantial account of a similar show mounted on the Fucine Lake by the Emperor Claudius. The lake was fenced off, bleachers erected for the crowds, and two fleets provided, representing "Rhodians" and "Sicilians." Though the ships at first avoided each other, they were eventually forced to fight, and provided an agreeable amount of slaughter. The entertainment was marred by the collapse of the bank, attributed to the fact that Claudius' minister had skimped on the construction to permit him to pocket the funds.

The most famous site for such spectacles in Rome was, of course, the Flavian Amphitheatre, or Colosseum, begun by Vespasian and dedicated in A.D. 80 by his successor, Titus. It stood on ground once occupied by the "Golden House," the fabulous palace built by Nero out of the shambles of the fire of Rome. The Flavians, seeking to mark a clean break with the hated dynasty that they superseded, replaced Nero's monument with public works. Part of the palace became a foundation for public baths. The colossal statue of Nero, from which the popular name of the amphitheatre derived, was given a new face. Martial writes of the scaffolding rising around the new structure, and celebrates with politic fervor the fact that "what was once their lord and master's pleasure is now given to the people."

As a practical gesture toward better public relations, the Colosseum was superb, though modern critics tend to reverse Martial's verdict, finding that the Golden House represented a more civilized taste. The new amphitheatre stood in the bed of Nero's artificial lake. This permitted the laying of a deep concrete foundation and also facilitated the flooding of the arena for water spectacles. The latter practice was, however, soon abandoned: the task of drying out the arena became tiresome, and the sea fights were transferred to more convenient locations.

The building itself was constructed largely from stone salvaged from the Golden House, with the outer walls rising in four solid tiers. It was designed to handle huge and often fractious crowds, with a capacity of some fifty thousand. There were originally eight numbered entrances, leading to interior staircases which gave access to each level separately. Women were restricted by imperial decree to the upper tiers, with the lower levels reserved for dignitaries who were protected from the beasts and missiles by a permanent wall and a removable fence of gilt metal adorned with elephant's tusks. Under the arena lay a warren of cells, corridors, and cages, to provide both for stage machinery of the type Seneca describes, and counterweighted elevators to convey the animals to the surface. Similar arrangements are found in the amphitheatres of Pozzuoli (Roman Puteoli) and Capua: the substructure of the latter is simpler than that of the Colosseum, with a wide central corridor giving access to small cells on either side. In some respects, Capua seems positively luxurious: an underground fountain provided running water, while the gladiators could await their entrance in a "greenroom" at ground level.

Suetonius records the lavish displays which opened the Colosseum. Apart from the usual display of gladiators, there were sea fights staged in the artificial lake built by Augustus; this was afterward drained to hold a *venatio* in which 5,000 animals were despatched in a single day's slaughter. Martial's running commentary on the entertainments in the Colosseum shows how heavily the amphitheatre now leaned upon the stage. One spectacle offered elaborate moving scenery, with "sliding cliffs and a miraculous and moving wood, such as men believed the grove of the Hesperides to be." Various wild beasts and birds were introduced into this setting, together with a victim dressed as Orpheus, whose music lamentably failed to charm the beasts: the show ended with Orpheus being mangled by an "ungrateful bear." Another poem alludes to a victim dressed as Daedalus, who also made his exit from life pursued by a bear. "How you must wish you had your wings now!" is Martial's callous comment.

From other poems we learn of the variety of the hunts. The bulls are enraged by straw dummies (*pila*) thrown into the arena. One bull is matched with a rhinoceros; another is described as it rises on the elevator, "borne aloft from the arena's midst, and

Capua, Roman amphitheatre, showing subterranean passages for beasts and combatants.

mounting to the skies." A bear is caught, like birds, with nets and lime. We hear of famous beast fighters, notably Carpophorus, who is compared to Hercules, and was perhaps so costumed: he killed a boar, a bear, and a leopard in succession. A water show is described, with a boat rowed by a crew dressed as Nereids, possibly by artificial light.

Such activities continued into the declining years of the capital. In the later Empire, acrobats regularly performed in the middle of the charging beasts. A bas-relief from Africa shows a naked woman straddling a bull with her hands tied behind her back, while a panther leaps at her. She may be forcibly enacting the myth of the Theban Dirke, who met her death in such a manner, or the rape of Europa. Apuleius, mystic, traveler, and novelist of the second century A.D., gives in his *Metamorphoses* (*The Golden Ass*) an account of a spectacle which, though fictional, may be taken as evidence for the entertainment of the time, in which ballet was mixed with slaughter and performing animals with pantomime. The show begins with formation dancing, in which a company of boys and girls present the old Greek Pyrrhic, or war dance. Then

when the trumpet signaled the end of the winding and convoluted movements of the dance, the curtain was removed, the hangings rolled aside, and the scene revealed.

It was a mountain built of wood to represent that famous Mount Ida of which the poet Homer sang, an imposing man-made structure covered with turf and living trees. The designer had contrived a stream that opened on the summit and poured its water down the mountainside. Here and there, she-goats were cropping the grass, with a young man playing the goatherd dressed as Paris the Phrygian shepherd, in flowing Asiatic robes with a gold tiara on his head. Then entered a handsome boy, naked except for the cloak of youth over his left shoulder, with striking yellow hair from which emerged little golden wings. His wand and winged staff showed him to be Mercury. Dancing toward Paris, he presented him with a golden apple, explaining in mime that these were Jupiter's instructions: he then beat a graceful retreat and vanished from sight. He was followed by a girl with admirable features who represented Juno, with a white diadem on her head and a sceptre in her hand. Then another girl came running in; you could tell she was Minerva by the shining helmet on her head and the coronet of olive-leaves upon it, and the way she brandished her shield and spear as though about to do battle. Yet another girl broke in upon them, whose outstanding beauty and ambrosial complexion proclaimed her to be Venus.

Each goddess has her train of attendants and offers an appropriate dance; Venus is accompanied by a *corps de ballet* dressed as Cupids, carrying bows and arrows and wedding torches. The Judgement of Paris follows, with Juno and Minerva miming their anger at being rejected, while Venus performs a sensuous dance of triumph. At this point "a fountain of wine mixed with saffron spurted from a hidden pipe on the mountain-top, falling in a perfumed shower on the browsing goats . . . till the whole theatre reeked of the fragrance. The earth gaped, and swallowed up the wooden mountain." The crowd now shouts for a different sort of spectacle, the coupling of a female prisoner with a donkey, after which the victim is to be eaten by wild beasts. A *venatio* is planned for the finale.

The growing power of Christianity gradually suppressed such spectacles. Provoked by attacks on their religion from the stage, the early Christian writers retaliated with moral outrage and threat of hell-fire. Gladiatorial shows were abolished in 404, to the disgust of the populace, and *venationes* in 523. The Colosseum, the theatre for hunting, as Cassius Dio had described it, became a showplace of Christian martyrdom, and began to acquire the aura of spurious legend with which it is still surrounded. Even in the Middle Ages and the Renaissance, however, it could still occasionally be put to its old uses: Christian plays were given there which seem to have preferred, perhaps by association, the bloodier episodes of Biblical stories, and a bullfight was held in which several noble Romans were killed. Amphitheatres elsewhere in the Empire have similarly preserved memories of the *venationes* to the present day: that at Nîmes, for example, still in good condition, is used regularly for bullfights. In one way at least the amphitheatres influenced the staging of the medieval drama. The idea of human combat preserved in chastened form in the hippodromes of Byzantium helped to influence the medieval tournament, which, like the *venationes* of antiquity, often assumed a dramatic guise and was staged in arenas whose shape the Romans would have recognized.

The Christian writers were by no means unanimous in their disapproval of the serious drama. Several of them indeed, proposed that it should be revived or introduced elements of it into their own presentations. In their learned squabbles we may discern the survival both of the plays themselves and the peripheral arts for some centuries. Athens remained the home of polite comedy. Antioch, in Syria, regarded as the nursery of actors, was an important dramatic center, staging revivals of Euripides, Menander, and even, curiously, Aristophanes. An account of the world prepared for the Emperor Constantius states that the best actors come from Tyre and Beirut, the best pantomimes from Caesarea, the best teachers from Gaza, and the best rope dancers from Castaretia. Performances lingered longest in the Eastern Empire, where Greek influence was still all-pervasive. In the West, the plays survived largely as reading texts with the manner of performance either faultily remembered or totally forgotten. Although the Renaissance brought major revivals of Seneca, Plautus, and Terence, Greek drama continued to languish in obscurity: though we hear of occasional school performances intended more as aids to the study of the text than as dramatic events in their own right. Greek drama did not return to the living theatre repertory until the closing years of the nineteenth century.

Selected Bibliography

Ancient Sources

For those without knowledge of the ancient languages, access to primary sources is difficult, as some have never been translated. There is, for example, no complete English version of Pollux, or of the scholia to the Greek tragedies and comedies. The following works, from which much of the material in the preceding chapters has been drawn, are easily obtainable in English:

Cicero. *De Oratore,* together with *De Fato* and others. E. W. Sutton and H. Rackham (trs.). The Loeb Classical Library. Cambridge, Mass.: Harvard University Press, 1942.

Lucian. *On the Dance.* In *Lucian.* A. M. Harmon (tr.). The Loeb Classical Library. New York: G. P. Putnam's Sons, 1913; London: Heinemann, 1913–1967.

Nagler, Alois M. *Sources of Theatrical History.* New York: Theatre Annual, 1952. (Contains translations of key passages from Pollux, Vitruvius, and others.)

Quintilian. *Institutio Oratoria.* H. E. Butler (tr.). The Loeb Classical Library. New York: G. P. Putnam's Sons, 1913; London: Heinemann, 1921–1936.

Vitruvius. *De Architectura.* M. H. Morgan (tr.). Cambridge, Mass.: Harvard University Press, 1914.

Modern Works

Arnott, Peter. *Greek Scenic Conventions in the Fifth Century B.C.* Oxford: Clarendon Press, 1962.

——. *An Introduction to the Greek Theatre.* London: Macmillan, 1959; New York: St. Martin's Press, 1959.

Beare, William. *The Roman Stage.* 3rd ed. New York: Barnes & Noble, 1963.

Bieber, Margarete. *The History of the Greek and Roman Theater.* 2nd ed. Princeton, N.J.: Princeton University Press, 1961.

Duckworth, George. *The Nature of Roman Comedy.* Princeton, N.J.: Princeton University Press, 1952.

Flickinger, Roy. *The Greek Theater and Its Drama.* Chicago: University of Chicago Press, 1936.

Haigh, A. E. *The Attic Theatre.* 3rd ed. by Sir Arthur Pickard-Cambridge. New York: Haskell House Ltd., 1968.

Hanson, John. *Roman Theater-Temples.* Princeton, N.J.: Princeton University Press, 1959.

Lawler, Lillian. *The Dance in Ancient Greece.* Middletown, Conn.: Wesleyan University Press, 1965.

Pickard-Cambridge, Sir Arthur. *The Dramatic Festivals of Athens.* Oxford: Clarendon Press, 1953.

——. *The Theatre of Dionysus in Athens.* Oxford: Clarendon Press, 1946.

Sifakis, G. M. *Studies in the History of Hellenistic Drama.* London: Athlone Press, 1967.

Webster, T. B. L. *Greek Theatre Production.* 2nd ed. London: Methuen, 1970.

Index

About the Author

PETER D. ARNOTT is currently Professor of Drama at Tufts University. He received his B.A. from the University of Wales and from Oxford University and his M.A. and Ph.D. from the University of Wales. Prior to coming to Tufts, he taught at the University of Iowa. As a performer and interpreter of Greek drama Professor Arnott has visited numerous campuses throughout the United States and Canada. He is a frequent contributor to scholarly journals, and he has translated many Greek and Roman plays. He is the author of several books including *An Introduction to the Greek Theatre* (1959), *Greek Scenic Conventions* (1961), *The Theatres of Japan* (1969), and *An Introduction to the Roman World* (1970).

F

I